Time Management

In the age of Work From Home and Hybrid Era

K W Patton

© Copyright 2022 - All rights reserved.

The content contained within this book may not be reproduced, duplicated or transmitted without direct written permission from the author or the publisher.

Under no circumstances will any blame or legal responsibility be held against the publisher, or author, for any damages, reparation, or monetary loss due to the information contained within this book, either directly or indirectly.

Legal Notice:

This book is copyright protected. It is only for personal use. You cannot amend, distribute, sell, use, quote or paraphrase any part, or the content within this book, without the consent of the author or publisher.

Disclaimer Notice:

Please note the information contained within this document is for educational and entertainment purposes only. All effort has been executed to present accurate, up to date, reliable, complete information. No warranties of any kind are declared or implied. Readers acknowledge that the author is not engaged in the rendering of legal, financial, medical or professional advice. The content within this book has been derived from various sources. Please consult a licensed professional before attempting any techniques outlined in this book.

By reading this document, the reader agrees that under no circumstances is the author responsible for any losses, direct or indirect, that are incurred as a result of the use of the information contained within this document, including, but not limited to, errors, omissions, or inaccuracies.

Table of Contents

Table of Contents

Introduction

Chapter 1: Why Work From Home?

  Working From Home and Productivity

  What's the Difference?

    Less Time Spent Traveling

    Fewer Distractions From Colleagues

    More Time for Yourself

  Disadvantages of Working From Home

    Distractions

    Lack of Social Interactions

    Security Concerns

    Lack of Office Equipment

    Self-Regulation

    Lack of Motivation

    Difficulty With Teamwork

- Burnout
- Advantages of Working From Home
  - It Saves Money
  - You Get to Customize Your Space
  - No Commuting
  - Fewer Things to Worry About
  - Better Work/Life Balance
  - Fewer Distractions
  - Flexible Schedule
  - A Positive Impact on Your Health
- Chapter 2: Create a Workspace
  - Things to Consider When Setting up a Workspace
    - Picking the Right Spot
    - The Importance of Height
    - Getting the Right Chair
    - Proper Lighting
    - Internet Service
    - Other Equipment and Accessories

A Digital Workspace

   The Advanced To-Do List

      Pros and Cons of the Advanced To-Do Lists

   The Kanban Method

      Pros and Cons of the Kanban Method

   "Rows, Columns, n' Sheets" Method

      Pros and Cons of the "Rows, Columns, n' Sheets" Method

   Team-Based Productivity

      Pros and Cons of Team-Based Productivity Method

Chapter 3: Minimize Distractions

Common Distractions When Working From Home

   Family

   Television

   The Internet

   Chores

   Food

- Pets
- How to Avoid Distractions
  - Keeping It Separate
  - Switch Off Notifications
  - Log Out of Social Media
  - Take Breaks
  - Reward Yourself
  - Acceptance

Chapter 4: Plan Ahead and Prepare a Schedule

- Why Is a Schedule Important for Working From Home?
- Tips for Scheduling Your Day
  - Plan the Day/Night Before
  - Prioritize
  - Add Exercise to Your Schedule
  - Don't Forget Your Breaks
  - Get Tedious Tasks Out of the Way
  - Use Management Tools to Help
  - Stop Working at the End of the Workday

The Ideal Work-From-Home Schedule

Email Management

    Create Email Checkpoints

    Quick Replies Come First

    Organize Your Mailbox

    Use Filters

    Implement a Time Limit

Exercise: Create Your own Schedule

Chapter 5: Setting Goals and Staying Motivated

The Benefits of Setting Goals

    Increased Productivity

    Creativity and Innovation

    Fewer Missed Workdays

    Improved Skills

    Rewards

How to Develop Measurable Goals

1. Identify Your Goals
2. Break Down Goals Into Smaller Tasks

3. Schedule Accordingly

4. Review and Adapt as Necessary

SMART Goals

Dress the Part

How to Plan Your Work Wardrobe

Chapter 6: Know Your Forte

Why It's Good to Know Your Strengths

Increases Productivity

Boosts Self-Confidence

Improves the Way You Engage With Your Work

Increased Retention Among Team Members

How to Identify Your Work Strengths

Ask Others

Think About What You Enjoy Doing

Relationship Style

When Are You in the Zone?

Pay Attention When You Ask for Help

Name Your Strengths

- Take a Test

Chapter 7: Unplug and Switch Off

- Why Unplug?
  - Unplugging Helps You Stop Working
  - It Benefits Your Mental Health
  - Improves Relationships
  - It Helps You Sleep Better
  - It Helps You Be More Productive During Work Hours
- How to Switch off at the End of the Day
  - Develop Clear Boundaries
  - Move Away From Your Workspace
  - Have a Shutdown Ritual
  - Choose a Hobby
  - Run Errands
  - Decrease Screen Time
  - Choose to Be Mindful
  - Engage With Friends and Family
  - Practice Acceptance

Conclusion

References

Introduction

People are more productive working at home than people would have expected. Some people thought that everything was just going to fall apart, and it hasn't. – Mark Zuckerberg

In 2015, I embarked on a new journey—working from home. I accepted a new position within my company that offered me the opportunity to be a remote worker. I ended up saying **goodbye to** daily commutes and office distractions. However, working from home is not a simple transition. It comes with its own set of trials and tribulations that people don't realize until they try it for themselves. Many people have discovered this in recent years as a result of the Covid-19 pandemic. Working remotely is entirely different from bringing work home occasionally. It is a lifestyle change—one that takes some time to master if you are just starting out. It took me a while to learn what needed to be done to maintain my productivity levels and ensure that I had a healthy work/life balance. Even though the pandemic also affected my working style, it was easy for me to adapt because I knew the core principles of time management and working from home. This is what I want to share with you in this book.

Working from home was once considered something people did between jobs. We have been conditioned to believe that going to work every day means getting up, going to an office, and sitting through meetings before it's time to go home. It is easy to lose time during the work day when you get distracted by colleagues, email notifications, and meetings that take way too long to finish. Thus, many people end up taking work home just to be able to complete it on time. Working from home in this manner is undesirable as you learn to despise it for taking up your personal time. If you have this mindset, it may make the transition to working from home even harder.

Times have changed drastically in recent years, making it possible to work from anywhere. Many companies across the globe have embraced the concept of remote working as they have realized the benefits of doing so. It has allowed them to find experienced employees and decrease their overhead costs. Companies don't have to worry about paying a fortune for office space, utilities, furniture, and equipment. Likewise, workers also benefit from saving money as well because they don't have to worry about paying for daily commutes, food costs, and even clothing expenses. We often don't realize how these costs add up because it all feels like a part of our daily work routine.

It does not matter what your reason is for working from home, you will be able to experience a multitude of benefits. Many people have successfully made the transition because they want a better quality of life, better jobs without having to move to different cities, or the freedom to move without having to give up their ideal job. However, failing to manage your time effectively when working remotely may shroud these benefits in negativity. You may feel guilty or unhappy because you are failing to be productive at home or unable to meet deadlines because of endless distractions. I can guarantee you this is not because you are not cut out for remote work. You just haven't figured out the right way to manage your time and productivity. I know this because I was also in the exact same position when I started. It wasn't until I changed my mindset toward working entirely that I was able to work from home successfully. Now, I'm even able to travel and still maintain my work schedule and productivity. This is something that you can do, too, with the right guidance. Working from home can be fulfilling, lucrative, and can definitely improve your mental and physical health. I have discovered six main steps to follow to achieve this and will share them in this book.

There is no major secret involved, it just takes time to learn these steps through personal experience, and most people do not have the luxury of time. During the start of the pandemic, people were thrown into the proverbial deep end and learned how to survive working at home while simultaneously dealing with family, noisy neighbors, pets, and other distractions. There was no time to learn, everyone was just trying to survive uncertain times and keep their jobs. It wasn't just normal office workers either. Even celebrities had to start working from home to maintain some sort of normalcy. Musicians set up home studios, talk show hosts like Jimmy Fallon, James Cordon, and Trevor Noah started streaming their shows from home, and even actors did interviews from their homes. People had an understanding and laughed off any disturbances in the background. However, things are changing again. The understanding people had is now gone and working from home requires crucial time management. I have spent the last seven years learning to manage my time effectively, and I want to share these methods with you. It will enable you to manage your time, successfully work from home, and help you build the working life that you are comfortable with. No more burnouts, no more missing important family events, and no more missing deadlines.

Managing your time effectively while working from home means setting clear boundaries. It can be easy to lose track of work and home life when there is no physical barrier between the two. Therefore, you have to ensure that you keep these boundaries clear to yourself and others while maintaining a healthy balance. When this is done, you will find that you can increase your productivity at work by remaining focused and less susceptible to distractions. In turn, this will also improve your quality of work. You will quickly find that when you learn to manage your time better, you will learn your true potential when it comes to working. You will be able to set meaningful goals and achieve targets that seemed impossible before. So, are you ready to learn how to manage your time and excel at working remotely? There are six steps that I have identified as being the core principles of working at home. These are creating a workspace, minimizing distractions, creating a schedule, setting goals, knowing your strengths, and learning to unplug. I will not just guide you through them but also explain how they can help you and why they are so important. This will allow you to understand them and implement them quickly without being left with questions. Let's get started!

Chapter 1: Why Work From Home?

Before we jump into the six steps of time management, I wanted to go through the aspects of working from home and why it has become more mainstream in recent years. Everyone has different reasons for contemplating a work-from-home lifestyle. Although many companies do not offer employees the opportunity to work from home permanently, more of them are opening up to the idea of a hybrid working situation. This means that employees could spend a few days in the office and then work from home for the rest. In fact, this is what most companies have implemented as they have people returning to the office after working from home during the pandemic. Statistics show that in the United States alone, almost 4.7 million people work remotely about 50% of the time, and approximately 16% of companies hire remote workers only (Apollo Technical, 2021).

During the height of the Covid-19 pandemic, people who worked non-essential jobs had no option but to work from home. Companies could either allow employees to work from home or had to shut down until the lockdown period passed. Unfortunately, many companies that chose the latter response did not survive this period or had to resort to massive staff cuts to make it through. In contrast, those companies that allowed employees to work from home were pleasantly surprised to find that the idea of employees working from home was actually not that bad. They saved money on overheads, and everyone could work from the comfort of their own home. Employees also noticed the immediate benefits of not having to get up early to get to the office on time and avoiding peak hour traffic. It's amazing how much more energy you have in a day if you haven't spent it frustrated in morning traffic! That was one of the first things I noticed when I started working from home. There was an immediate impact on my mental and physical health.

Working from home has also been driven by advances in technology. Technology has made it much easier for people to connect. It doesn't matter where you are in the world. As long as you have a good internet connection, you can dial into a meeting or review a company document while online. It has even made it possible for companies to hire people in a completely different country, expanding workforces and increasing diversity in the workplace. However, despite these obvious advantages, 44% of companies in the United States do not offer work-from-home options (Apollo Technical, 2021). While some industries, like food production and car manufacturers, cannot have employees working from home, some are reluctant because they fear a decrease in productivity levels. It is easy to think that working from home will result in a reduction in productivity because there is no one watching and there are more distractions. This, however, is very rarely true. Working from home usually leads to an increase in productivity, and where there is a decrease, it is generally because of specific situations or barriers to working. This is what we will go through next.

Working From Home and Productivity

A person's productivity levels are dependent on many things. It's not just about their location but also their ability to focus and their time management skills. Everybody is different, and it is, therefore, hard for companies to tell how things will turn out with regard to productivity. You can't really blame them for being hesitant to offer employees the opportunity to work from home. However, a recent study conducted by Owl Labs reported that there is an increase in productivity of 13% for people who work from home and 77% for those who work remotely (Apollo Technical, 2022). It should be noted, though, that these percentages are in a world coming out of a global pandemic.

Prior to the pandemic, the productivity levels of employees working from home depended on the type of work they were given. If it was a boring task, then employees tended to complete it faster in the office than at home. This was attributed to being easier to procrastinate at home than at the office. However, if the task was something that was more on the creative side or more appealing to the employee, they would complete it faster. Furthermore, if all employees from a single office decided to work from home, they tended to underperform. This is because they base their level of productivity on others. No one wanted to be highly productive if they knew others were shirking off (Glenn Dutcher, 2012). Needless to say, mindsets have shifted since 2012. The Covid-19 pandemic saw many people having to work from home. It also changed perspectives with regard to productivity levels. Employees were able to increase productivity when working from home by up to 47% in 2020 when compared to 2019 (Prodoscore, 2020).

This drastic change is hardly surprising. Not only has technology advanced considerably in recent years, but necessity drove people to find ways to work from home efficiently. Even among the chaos of everyone being at home at the same time, they knew that they had to work. Companies were also more understanding of noisy backgrounds, and some even introduced flexible working hours to help employees cope. In most of these cases, productivity levels went up. Employers noticed that their staff were able to get more work done in shorter periods of time. This led them to question if working from home was the path they should pursue in the future. If they could save money on office overheads and employees were performing better, why should they return to working in an office? This is why many companies have allowed a hybrid working setup where employees can work from home on some days and come to the office on others. Some have even embraced employees working from home permanently and only coming to the office if absolutely necessary. In situations like these, companies found that paying employees for home office equipment and furniture was still cheaper than office rental space and utilities!

What's the Difference?

So, why does productivity increase when working from home and not in the office? Let's take a closer look at some of the main factors that boost productivity at home.

Less Time Spent Traveling

It does not matter how long your morning and evening commute is; it still sets the tone for your day. If you get stuck in morning traffic on the way to work, chances are you will be tired and irritable when you get to work. Likewise, if the same happens on your way home, you will probably not be in the best of moods when you arrive. Working from home eliminates daily commutes. Firstly, this means that workers can start work on time or even start earlier because they don't have to go anywhere. Secondly, employees will have higher energy levels and be in a better state of mind when they begin their workday. Lastly, fewer people traveling is also good for the environment. You can decrease your carbon footprint simply by using your car or public transport less.

Fewer Distractions From Colleagues

Colleagues are a source of major distractions in the office. Whether you work in a cubicle or have your own office, someone stopping by to drop something off or even passing by can take up a huge chunk of time. While it may seem like taking a break and just having a laugh, it can quickly translate into you falling behind on the task you are working on. When you are working from home, this doesn't happen and allows you to work without losing focus. Even if work colleagues try to chat with you via email or a messaging service, you don't have to respond immediately. However, if they're standing in front of you in the office, you can't exactly dodge them.

More Time for Yourself

When working from home, you will quickly realize that you end up with more time for yourself. You don't have to get up early, so you can choose to get more sleep or use this time to exercise. During your lunch break, you don't have to worry about rushing around, and you can use this time to do something around the house. During the pandemic, people took up gardening, baking, and cooking because they were at home and had the time. This all contributes to a healthy work/life balance and can greatly improve your health. In turn, this all leads to better performance at work due to a more balanced lifestyle.

These are just the main factors that improve productivity when working from home. They all revolve around having more time to work and live the way that you want to. As much as this is great news, not everyone has the same experience when working from home. I'm here to tell you that it is okay if you struggle when working from home. It's not always an easy transition, and it is normal if you initially struggle with maintaining your productivity level. I have been in your position, and it is also one of the main reasons I wanted to write this book. It is possible for you to also enjoy working from home. You just have to gain an understanding of why you are struggling, and then you will be able to take the necessary steps to improve your situation.

Disadvantages of Working From Home

It is often easier to identify the advantages of working from home than to consider the disadvantages. However, by understanding these disadvantages better, you will be able to adapt better to working from home. This is because you will be able to tell which areas you need to work on.

Distractions

It is easy to get distracted when you are working from home. Family can sometimes cause major distractions unintentionally. Your partner might ask you for help, the kids may want to know what you are doing, or your pets might want some attention. However, even beyond these, since you are at home, you also have to fight other temptations. Television, online shopping, and deliveries can tempt you away from work easily when no one is watching. There's no such thing as having the television on in the background while you work because sooner or later, you will get distracted.

Lack of Social Interactions

Sometimes, working from home can get lonely. If you live by yourself and your home is quiet while you work, you may also have difficulty focusing. It is also easy to start missing your colleagues at work. Even if you still communicate with them, it is rather different from seeing them in person. This can affect your mental health and your attitude towards working from home.

Security Concerns

Depending on the type of job you have, you may have concerns about the way documents are shared when working remotely. As much as technology has made it easier to stay connected, it has also left us susceptible to cyber crimes. Therefore, if your concerns are not properly addressed by your company, you may be hesitant to work from home and will feel more comfortable back in the office.

Lack of Office Equipment

It can be challenging to work from home without the proper equipment. Not everyone can afford a home office with printers, large computer screens, ergonomic chairs, and keyboards. You can be comfortable working on your couch for a day or two, but after a few weeks, your back will start reminding you why you like your chair at work.

Self-Regulation

Not everyone can work well on their own. Working from home means you have to be in charge of your working hours and what you do in that time. This is often easier said than done. You don't have to be reminded to work when you are in an office setting. You know that you have to. However, when you are at home, you have to be able to use your time efficiently.

Lack of Motivation

When you don't get to connect with your team or manager in person, you may lack motivation. We often don't realize how much encouragement we receive at work until it is taken away. When colleagues see you having a hard time or notice that you are struggling, they can motivate you to get through a difficult project. This is harder to do when everyone is working from home. It is easier to hide your struggles from a distance, and it makes it harder for others to help. Learning and practicing self-motivation can help, but it is often not as effective as hearing it from others. This is when communication comes in.

Difficulty With Teamwork

Although it is easy to connect with team members through various platforms, sometimes it makes it much harder to work with them. This is because not everyone on the team may be fully invested in the virtual meeting. Maybe they have external distractions that are keeping them from being involved, or maybe they are just tired of online meetings. There are some teams who work better when they are in a room together, bouncing ideas around. This is where hybrid working styles come in handy.

Burnout

The last disadvantage of working from home is the risk of burnout. It is possible to be a little too productive while working from home. Work can quickly take over if you do not have clear boundaries between work and home life. You have more time on your hands since you are working from home, and if you don't use that time wisely, you could just continue working.

This is not something you should do continuously, as it will lead to eventual burnout. Furthermore, you don't want your home to be a place you begin to despise because of how much work you have. Work never ends. If it does, it means you're unemployed! No matter how much you do today, you will still have more tomorrow. Setting realistic goals will keep you on track and remind you when it's time to step away for the day.

These are the disadvantages of working from home. If you are experiencing any of these, don't worry. The steps I will discuss directly address these disadvantages by giving you ways to work around them. Before we dive into them, though, I also want to go through the advantages of working from home. This will give you a clear idea of what working from home can do for you.

Advantages of Working From Home

Time is the biggest advantage of working from home—which is why time management is so important. There are other important benefits to working from home as a consequence of being more productive and having more time.

It Saves Money

Think about it. If you didn't have to go to the office every day? Transport, food, coffee, work clothes, and even snacks add up quickly. I didn't realize how much money I spent on my morning coffee on the way to work. In fact, most Americans don't realize that if you stop buying coffee every morning, you could save between $1,000 and $2,000 a year (Rosen, 2020). With the current rising food and fuel costs, can you imagine how much money you could save by simply working from home? It is a massive advantage.

You Get to Customize Your Space

Sometimes, we need a little inspiration or comfort when working. This could be in the form of our favorite quotes, mementos, music, or maybe photos of our loved ones. However, an office or cubicle space may not allow for that.

You may even feel uncomfortable having your colleagues look through your things. When you work from home, you have the freedom to customize your space and have it exactly how you want it!

No Commuting

Yes. I will repeat it because this is how much of a benefit it is. Not having to commute to work every day is a massive advantage. You will be able to get proper rest without having to wake up early and not have to worry about getting home late because of traffic. Furthermore, your overall mood will improve. In addition, not commuting to work reduces your carbon footprint and that of your company significantly. Just look at how a reduction in traffic reduced greenhouse gasses and improved air quality in cities across the globe!

Fewer Things to Worry About

When we lead such busy lives, clearing any items from our to-do list is a great feeling. Imagine not having to get up early so that you have enough time to iron your clothes or do your makeup. You don't have to worry about these too much when you work from home. Also, things like stopping at the gas station in the evening so you don't get late in the morning or making it to your kid's concert. When you eliminate the rush of travel time, annoying colleagues who won't let you work, and figuring out when to fit in your workout, you end up with a clearer schedule and a less busy mind. Having fewer things to worry about clears out your mind and allows you to formulate ideas easily. This makes a huge difference to the way you work.

Better Work/Life Balance

If you work from home and have clear boundaries, you can enjoy a much better work/life balance. You will free up time that will allow you to spend more time with your family and friends, pursue new hobbies, and find time to work out. This all contributes to a more balanced life and not one in which all your energy is consumed by work.

Fewer Distractions

Being in an office makes it easier for you to get distracted or interrupted from working. Colleagues could be talking to each other loudly, they could want to show you their new cat, or you could get caught up in a conversation about last night's football. This takes away from your working time and makes it difficult to get back into the zone you were in before you were interrupted. Furthermore, you might find it difficult to make calls to clients and have to find a quiet meeting room or step outside. Working from home eliminates these noisy distractions and makes it easier to make phone calls.

Flexible Schedule

Working from home and managing your time efficiently will allow you to have a flexible schedule. Managers usually don't have issues with employees stepping out for an appointment or doing school pick-ups if they show that they can manage their time properly and maintain productivity. This gives you more to get things done that you would usually try to cram into the weekends or get others to do for you. I have learned that I can even work remotely while traveling as I can divide my time appropriately.

A Positive Impact on Your Health

Working from home can have a massive impact on your physical and mental health. Firstly, your energy levels will be better, allowing you to pursue other activities and exercise. Secondly, you will also find yourself eating healthier because it's easy to look for snacks at work when energy levels dip in the afternoons. At home, you can choose healthier snacks and eliminate junk food from the house to avoid temptations. Thirdly, your mood will improve because you won't be tired all the time, nor will the thought of work be shrouded in negativity. Fourthly, living a healthier lifestyle will also mean fewer sick days. Lastly, when you get to see how nicely everything in your life comes together, it gives you a sense of contentment. We all strive for happiness, and leading a healthy, balanced lifestyle contributes greatly to making this happen.

So, as you can see, working from home has both advantages and disadvantages. However, more people are opting to work from home because of the benefits listed above. They don't experience the disadvantages because, like me, they have learned ways to eliminate them and shift their mindsets. This is what we will move on to next. By following six easy steps, you can also experience all these benefits and genuinely enjoy working from home. It all starts with taking the first step and creating your workspace.

Chapter 2: Create a Workspace

The first step to successfully working from home is to create a space to work from. It does not have to be a complete home office if you don't have a spare room or study. You just need a dedicated workspace that will mimic a work setting and put you in the right state of mind. Thus, by simply stepping into your workspace, you will know it is time to get to work. Setting up a workspace is easy once you know what it should include. It's not just about the furniture and equipment either. You have to think about stationary, software, and how the setup affects your home. Extension cords running across high-traffic areas in a household are just asking for trouble, and even though using your home phone may seem convenient, keeping track of the separate costs is tricky.

A workspace at home requires some thought. If you do not have a room to use as an office, you should choose a quiet area in your home where you won't be easily distracted. For example, setting up your workspace in the dining or living room is not a good idea if that's where your family spends most of their time. Keeping things separate will help you stay focused. A workspace is not just about having your laptop and an internet connection either. We often don't realize how much thought goes into an office plan because it's already set up when we start our jobs. Working from home will teach you that there are quite a few things you need to have to make your work life at home easier.

Things to Consider When Setting up a Workspace

With this section, I have put together a list of things you need for a home office or workspace. It isn't about going out and buying a ton of stuff but highlighting the requirements that will make the most significant impact. These form the core elements of a good workspace.

Picking the Right Spot

Although I did mention this earlier, let's go into the details of finding the right spot for your workspace. Firstly, using a study, guest room, garage, or even an enclosed balcony is a great idea for a workspace. Having a door that separates these from busier areas can give you the separation you need between your work and living spaces. Therefore, one you enter this office and close the door, you will not get distracted, and your family will be less likely to come into your office because they know you are working.

However, if you do not have a spare room, then you have to find a dedicated space to set up your workspace. In this instance, you want to avoid living areas where you know your family spends time during the day. You don't want to be distracted by a television or the sound of the blender in the kitchen. Neither do you want to disrupt your family's daily routine. Having them stay quiet just so that you can have an online meeting is just as bad as them interrupting you.

Even if you live alone, you still want to set up your workspace in an area free from distractions. Windows can offer both relief and distraction. So if you want to be near a window, choose carefully and avoid windows that face a busy street. Pick an area where you have enough space for your desk, chair, and office equipment. You also want to ensure that you have adequate plug points and that you can move around a bit. The worst thing you can do is set up your workspace in a dark corner that you have to squeeze into. You want to enjoy your workspace, not hate it!

The Importance of Height

Did you know that there is an industry standard for working desk height? This is why office furniture looks so uniform. Desks are usually between 28 and 30 inches in height and are ideal for people around six ft in height (Greg, 2021). However, not everybody is the same height. This is why some people are comfortable at their desks while others battle. Creating your own workspace allows you to customize your desk for your height and comfort. Ideally, you want the height of your desk to be the same height as your elbow when you sit down. If you have a pull-out tray for your keyboard and mouse, then this should be elbow height, and your screen can be placed on the desk. You also want to make sure that you sit, your feet touch the ground, and the tops of your thighs don't touch the underside of the desk.

The other important factor is to ensure that your computer screen is at the right height. Many people prefer buying large screens that can be placed on a stand to get the ideal height. This prevents you from looking down at your laptop and straining your neck. It also keeps your shoulders squared and prevents you from hunching over.

Getting the Right Chair

The chair you use is one of the most crucial decisions you make in your workspace. It is easy just to take any comfortable chair from your home and use it as a desk chair. However, over time, you will find that these are not designed to be sat on for long periods of time. Your back will begin to hurt, and this will affect your productivity. You won't be able to focus on work if you are in pain. Thus, you should invest in an office chair that will provide comfort and support.

A good office chair is one that is adjustable, provides support for your lower back, and has wheels. With these features, you can adjust the height of the chair, the armrests, and the seat. In addition, the wheels will allow you to slip in and out from your desk without scraping against the floor. It is best to try out a chair first instead of just ordering one and hoping for the best. This will give a better idea of the specifications of the chair you need for your height and weight.

Proper Lighting

Lighting is often forgotten in a workspace at home. We all make the mistake of assuming that the lighting in the room is sufficient. If the lighting is not enough, most people go out and get a desk lamp. Both of these options are wrong. Firstly, the lighting in the room should not only be sufficient to light up your workspace, but the positioning of the light should not cause any unnecessary glare. The light should be overhead and should not reflect off your screen or be in your field of vision. This is why desk lamps are a bad idea. They cause a glare on your screen and can hurt your eyes because of the direct light.

The same thing goes for natural light coming in from windows. Natural lighting is great. However, it should never be directly behind you or to the side unless it is shaded by trees or curtains. Otherwise, when the sun shines through, it will make it difficult to see your screen. Adjusting the brightness of your screen is also vital to ensure the comfort of your eyes when working for long periods. However, this will differ for different people as eye sensitivity will vary.

Internet Service

The internet has made it easier to work from home. That being said, it can also be frustrating if it is problematic. You need a fast and reliable internet connection if you want to work from home. This is especially true if you tend to have frequent meetings or calls. It can come off as unprofessional if your internet keeps stalling during a meeting, and you have to ask people to repeat themselves or risk losing chunks of information because you missed what has been said. Thus, you should ensure that your internet service provider is reliable and can provide an internet speed of at least 50Mbps.

Other Equipment and Accessories

The requirements listed above are the most important elements of creating your workspace at home. However, there are other accessories that you can acquire that will make your work-at-home lifestyle easier. For example, a headset is an important thing to have for calls and meetings. You can also get noise-canceling ones now that will minimize background noises in your surroundings. Thus, if your neighbor's dogs are barking, other people won't be able to hear them when you are speaking.

Getting a keyboard, mouse, or touchpad is also a good idea if you purchase a larger screen. Using these external devices is easier than using the keyboard and touchpad on your laptop. Of course, this won't be necessary if you are working from a desktop PC. Also, even though we work primarily in digital format, having a multifunctional printer can come in handy. Sometimes you just cannot escape printing or scanning documents.

Another excellent investment for working from home is a surge protector or an uninterruptible power supply (UPS). This protects your computer from surges should the power go out.

You can also get a small UPS for your modem that will keep your internet running even if there is a blackout. However, this is limited by how long your laptop battery will last without charging. It is still a great option because it allows you to save your work and notify people that you will be unavailable instead of being immediately cut off.

If you like to listen to music when you work, then you can also invest in speakers. This will improve the quality of sound and save you from having to wear headphones all the time. A smart assistant is also not such a bad idea for a workspace. It will help you remember important meetings and calls in addition to saving your ideas for later. I often have a thought or idea while working and ask my smart assistant device to make a note for later. If an office assistant is not within the budget, a whiteboard can be just as effective. It will allow you to quickly jot down things to remember later or help you work on stuff visually. It can also help you be more productive if you use it to plan your day.

Another thing that's great to have in a workspace is a yoga mat. When you work from home, it's easy to get caught up for hours and forget to move around for a bit. This is why standing and treadmill desks have become so popular recently.

However, keeping a yoga mat nearby will remind you to stop and move your body for a few minutes. Even a few simple stretches can make all the difference, and your body will thank you for it. Plants are also a great mood booster to have in your workspace. Having plants will also encourage you to get up once in a while and water them or check on how they are growing.

A Digital Workspace

In addition to the physical items you need for a home workspace, you also need to be equipped with the right management tools that will help you keep track of your work and ensure that you are meeting deadlines. Fortunately, there are a variety of digital options to help you with this. However, before you choose your digital management tools, it is best to identify the management method that you want to use. There are a variety of management methods, and you should aim to choose the one that best suits your working style. I will go through three of the most popular methods and then describe the digital tools that complement the method.

The Advanced To-Do List

This method asks that you break down every aspect of your to-do list. It is extremely handy if you are working on multiple projects or just starting a project. You would create a list of the projects you are working on, and within each project, you would then list the tasks that you would have to complete. Taking it a step further, you would then assign information to each task. For example, if one of the tasks of the project was to write a quarterly report, you would then add a list of resources or documents you will be taking the information from. In this manner, when you actually set out to complete the task, you know exactly what needs to be done and how to do it. It can feel like too many lists, but if you like being organized and meticulous about your tasks, this can be a great method to use. However, you also should not spend more time making lists than actually working. The lists are there to help you, not to distract you from working.

There are many apps that can help you with these lists. Essentially, they are note-taking apps that help you make your lists. These apps function better than a simple notebook and pen by sorting out your projects and tasks in a way that's easy to understand and search. Thus, you won't have to spend hours trying to find the right document. These apps include Evernote, Notion, Google Keep, Microsoft OneNote, Obsidian, and Apple Notes.

Evernote

Evernote is one of the most popular note-taking apps and is compatible with Android and iOS devices. This is due to its accessibility, ease of use, and overall functionality. It allows you to store notes, images, documents, drawings, and scans, to name but a few. You just have to create a new note for your project and then place whatever you want into it. After that, you can assign tabs to this information. These tags will then act as sub-sections, and your information will be sorted according to these tags. Thus, you just have to click on a project and then navigate to the tag you want to see.

Evernote also has excellent search capabilities. If you upload a document or image with text, it will be able to pick up the text. So, if you search for a particular word regarding the image, it will read the text of the image and will be able to know what you are looking for. The functionality of this app will vary with the different subscription levels they have available.

Notion

You can use Notion for taking notes, listing tasks, and storing references. It is not just a great management tool but can also make collaboration with other colleagues easier. You can assign tasks to team members and can create checklists that can be ticked off when tasks have been completed. You can even separate your pages so that you have a private page for your work and a workspace that includes the pages you share with others. Thus, everything is kept separate, and your colleagues can't access your pages.

Google Keep

If you work on your Google Drive most of the time and use it for storage of all your work, Google Keep is an excellent app for your notes and lists. It links easily to all your devices, and you can save notes and images from all the Google apps you use. There is also a Chrome Extension available that facilitates this. Google Keep is a free app for the first 15GB. If you exceed this, then there is a fee for additional storage.

Microsoft OneNote

Microsoft OneNote is a favorite among many workers as it is a free app. It allows you to create digital notebooks that are broken down into pages. You have options to add to notes, images, and even handwritten notes if you have a stylus. It is a standard, no-frills app that will help you keep track of your work.

Obsidian

Obsidian is not a note-taking app that most people are familiar with. However, it is extremely useful and has many features that can help you keep track of your work. The great thing about Obsidian is that it allows you to create links between pages and notes. For example, you may already have written a report that can be used in an article you are currently writing. Thus, you can link that report to your notes for the article and be able to easily reference it when you write.

Apple Notes

Apple Notes are for users who are accustomed to Apple products. It is a free app but has the basic note-taking functionality that you need to create lists. One of the best features of this app is that you can link it to Siri and share notes with other Apple users. Apple Notes stores notes conveniently and allow you to search for them, but it will not sort these notes like some of the other apps on this list.

These note-taking apps are just some of the many available apps out there. They can help you create your advanced to-do lists in a way that keeps them organized and easy to follow. You will quickly find that they are much better than a stack of notes on your desk.

Pros and Cons of the Advanced To-Do Lists

The largest advantage of The Advanced To-Do List Method is that your tasks are easy to track. You don't have to worry about forgetting to do something because it is all documented. On the negative side, it can get confusing if you are unsure of how to set up the apps. Not everyone does well with to-do lists, and if they become too large, it can feel overwhelming.

The Kanban Method

The Kanban Method is great for people who need a visual of their progress. Remember how I said a whiteboard can be a good addition to your workspace? Well, the Kanban Method utilizes a whiteboard or corkboard to track the progress you make with your work. You need to divide the board into three sections representing the work that needs to be done, the work you are doing, and the work that you have completed. By using post-its, you can move your tasks over to each section. You can make it as elaborate as you like by color-coordinating clients or projects and by adding as much detail to the post-it as you require.

The Kanban Method can also be used digitally by using apps like LeanKit and Trello. They both use the same method to move tasks along as you complete them, allowing you to archive them when the project is complete. This method is also great for team projects because the entire team can track progress and see which tasks are holding up project completion.

Pros and Cons of the Kanban Method

The Kanban Method offers a visual aid for your projects and tasks. You can see the bigger picture clearly. Also, by color-coding your projects, you can easily see what's falling behind. The con with this method is that, unlike the previous method, it lacks specific details. Therefore, even though you can keep track of work, you still have to figure out what needs to be done for each task. When working in a team, this factor can be problematic.

"Rows, Columns, n' Sheets" Method

If you're the type of person that enjoys spreadsheets, this method is for you. Spreadsheets can be excellent management tools due to their functionality. You can create different sheets for different projects. Thereafter, you can utilize the rows and columns to list tasks and due dates. You can even take it one step further and use color formatting to rank the priority of the tasks.

Pros and Cons of the "Rows, Columns, n' Sheets" Method

In terms of this method, the pros and cons come down to whether you like using spreadsheets or not. It is simple and easy to use. However, if you don't like spreadsheets, you might find them time-consuming.

Team-Based Productivity

If your work is centered around teamwork, team-based productivity apps are what you need. These apps allow team members to track projects, delegate tasks and set due dates. The great thing about this is that it keeps everyone updated with any changes. Project managers can also see who is falling behind and reassign tasks if necessary.

Some of the team-based apps you can use include:

Trello

As mentioned earlier, Trello uses the Kanban Method. It provides a visual of project tasks and moves each card along as the work proceeds through different points towards completion. These cards can be assigned to team members, effectively allowing project managers to delegate tasks. You can also add colored tags to sort out the cards.

Asana

Asana is similar to Trello but allows you to choose how to visualize tasks. You can have a board view like Trello or change it to a list, calendar, or timeline view. In addition, you can assign due dates and break tasks up into subtasks.

Jira

Jira is an app that is tailored for software development teams. The tasks that need to be done are centralized in a backlog. This backlog can then be visualized as a Kanban Board or a Scrum Board. This app is not for everyone, as only those who understand agile development can use it efficiently.

Basecamp

Basecamp allows you to have different projects, and within these projects are categories where you can place team tasks. These categories include a message board, to-do lists, schedules, and a place to upload documents. In addition, Basecamp also has automatic check-ins that will provide an automatic progress report on the team's work. This eliminates the need for weekly check-in meetings.

Monday.com

The great thing about Monday.com is that it combines all the features of different management methods. It allows you to create boards for different projects, and these boards are then assigned rows and columns. This app also offers templates that save you from creating boards from scratch.

nTask

nTask is a great team-based app that has a time-tracking feature. This allows team members to start working on a task and keep track of the time taken for completion. In this manner, it eliminates the need for a separate timesheet. All projects can be broken down into tasks and to-do lists, ensuring that everyone knows what has to be done and by when.

Click Up

Click Up is similar to Asana in terms of how tasks can be viewed. However, Click Up allows you to define company goals and then link the tasks that will contribute to these goals. Thus, you can track your team's overall performance and which areas need to be addressed.

Pros and Cons of Team-Based Productivity Method

Using Team-based productivity apps is great for keeping a team updated and ensuring that tasks are completed on time. However, it can be costly depending on the size of your team and will take a bit of time to initially set up.

That sums up the management methods and apps you can use to set up your digital workspace. Remember, it's not just about the location of your workspace but also about having the right tools to ensure that you work well within the space. This will provide a solid foundation for you to maintain your productivity. The next step is to learn how to avoid distractions while working from home.

Chapter 3: Minimize Distractions

Many people got to experience working from home during the height of the pandemic. However, for most, it was a necessity and not a choice. There was no trying it out first, no time to adapt and to make matters worse, they also had to deal with the entire family being on lockdown. It's no surprise that a survey conducted on 1,000 employees in 2021 showed that 41.8% of them cited a decrease in overall life satisfaction (Mendoza, 2021). It wasn't the fact that they were working from home that caused this decrease but rather having to deal with the effects of the pandemic and subsequent lockdown period.

A lot of things happened in a short period of time that were both good and bad. Spouses and families were suddenly spending all their time together in their homes. As strange as it may sound, this was something that many were not accustomed to. From a busy life of constantly being on the move, everyone was suddenly grounded in one place. Some people handled it well, but the majority of us were at a loss as to how to survive being stuck inside. Then when you throw working from home in the mix, people either did the bare minimum at work and spent more time on chores or family; or they poured themselves into work as a coping mechanism and as a way to distract themselves from the chaos around them. Neither option was a good way to cope as any balance between work and home life was completely lost.

Thus, when people are questioned about working from home, they'd rather go back to work to regain some sort of balance. The damage, however, has already been done. According to the same survey, 41% of employees started work two hours earlier, and 59% said they worked well past the end of the work day (Mendoza, 2021). The major reasons for this were that they had to deal with household chores and homeschooling during the day. However, some of them also found it difficult to avoid watching television or playing video games to combat boredom and loneliness.

It's easy to see how working from home can be associated with negative implications for productivity and mental health, but we must also realize that the pandemic was an unprecedented time for us. Working from home can have positive outcomes when we learn how to do it properly. One of the major steps toward this is learning to minimize distractions. That was what people battled with during the pandemic. Whether they realized it or not, the distraction of everything else happening kept them from working, and the distraction of work kept them from living. Working from home is a fine balance, and you have to identify your distractions before you learn to avoid them.

Common Distractions When Working From Home

Distractions come in many shapes and forms. They have nothing to do with your attention span, nor are they an excuse for you not to work from home. You have nothing to feel bad about if you find yourself distracted. Everyone who has or is working from home experiences distraction. You just have to be able to recognize it for what it is and know how to deal with it. Research shows that irrespective of the type or duration of the interruption, it will take approximately 25 minutes to regain focus (Mark et al., 2008). This time can quickly add up, leading to feelings of being under pressure to finish on time, stress, and a decrease in productivity. Let's take a closer look at some of the most common distractions when working from home.

Family

Whether you live alone, with your partner, with your parents, or if you're a parent, family distractions are often hard to avoid. Even something as small as your partner asking what you want for lunch can lead to a 45-minute conversation about food and grocery shopping. Of course, they don't intend to be a distraction, but they can take away a lot of time from your work day. Each question, phone call, or story will take your focus away from what you are working on, and it will take time to regain this focus. This can lead to you working extra hours in an attempt to reach your daily goals and spending less quality time with your family overall.

This is probably one of the hardest distractions to navigate when working from home, as it's not just about putting up a physical barrier between your workspace and home life. You almost have to create mental and emotional barriers as well.

For example, you may feel like you are missing out when you can hear your kids telling your partner about their day when they get home from school. You may even feel guilty at times, but there are ways to work around this and get the best of both worlds.

Television

The television can be a huge distraction when working from home. People try to find excuses as to why the TV should be on. They say it provides background noise or that they have the news on, but it hardly ever works out well. Your workspace shouldn't even be anywhere close to the television unless you have no other choice. It has the ability to suck you into hours of frivolous entertainment. Whether it is your favorite TV show or an advertisement, they are designed to get you hooked so that you always want more. Thus, it is easy to lose large chunks of time to television without you even being aware.

You may think you are working, but the time taken to achieve your task will most likely be much longer. Furthermore, you could even produce work of sub-par quality because of your split focus. It is best to just imagine you are at the office and the television isn't even there. If you really need background noise, try playing music instead.

The Internet

The internet can be just as bad as the television when it comes to distractions—for some people, it actually may be harder to avoid the internet. This is because the internet bombards us with distractions constantly. Social media, online shopping, advertisements, funny videos, cute cat videos, email notifications—the list is endless. Since working from home entails using the internet, there's no distancing yourself from it. However, you have to find ways to disconnect from the distractions introduced.

There are multiple ways to do this, like disabling notifications and only checking emails at certain times or logging out of social media accounts while working. You will have to find the best option for you and the way you work.

Chores

When you're at the office, you will find yourself having random thoughts about what you need to do when you get home. However, when you work from home, you often have visual reminders. This stops it from being a random thought and makes it something that has to be done, and when you are working on a boring task, chores may seem more appealing and productive. There's nothing wrong with doing chores while you work from home, but you have to plan to do them the right way. Once you start with one household chore, it's easy to get caught up in a string of them and lose track of time.

If you want to tackle household chores without affecting your work day, learn how to schedule them into your day. In this manner, you can have a brain break from work and get some chores done. For example, you can put a load of clothes in the washer in the morning and then do some work before you have to transfer them to the dryer. You can even sweep your apartment if you need to move after sitting at your desk for a few hours. Just don't make household chores your only priority.

Food

Food can also be a persistent distraction when you work from home. When you work at an office, you usually have a packed lunch and snacks or go out and get something during your breaks. However, when you work from home, food is almost always available. Therefore, if you begin feeling a bit hungry, it's easy to head to the kitchen and grab something to snack on. This can easily become a distraction and also lead you to unhealthy eating habits. For example, you could grab a bag of chips from the pantry but then have difficulty eating them while working. Thus, you may abandon your keyboard for a while as you eat the chips. It could also lead you to prepare a whole meal when all you wanted was a snack.

You have to be prepared if you know that you can be easily distracted by food. You can prepare your meals in the morning or night before, try not to have junk food in the pantry, and only eat when you have scheduled a break.

Pets

If you have pets, you will find that they will want your attention when you are at home. This is because they don't understand you are working—they are just excited that you are with them! It can be hard to be mad at a dog that wants to play or a cat that thinks your keyboard is the ideal resting spot. However, you need to also draw boundaries with them so that they know that you are not available to play all day long.

The great thing about dogs is that you can come up with a routine that will help both of you. You can take your dog for a walk on your break or play with them in the backyard for a while. This can be a great way to get some exercise and fresh air while spending time with your dog. Cats generally fend for themselves, you will just have to learn to distract them so that they won't distract you. An interesting toy or treat can keep them occupied away from your workspace. You also should aim to get into the habit of saving your work often, just in case your pet decides to hit the wrong keys on your keyboard or pull on the wrong cord.

These distractions are just the most common ones, but by no means are they the only ones.

Cellphones, windows facing busy streets, noisy neighbors, and construction nearby can all act as distractions. However, the faster you learn to recognize a distraction, the faster you can learn to deal with them because you will be conscious of what they are doing. You don't want to have to work overtime or lose your ability to be productive within working hours because of distractions. Working from home is all about balance, and in the next section, I will guide you through finding that balance by learning to avoid distractions.

How to Avoid Distractions

Avoiding distractions takes practice. It is not something you can master immediately as you will have to adapt it to your unique situations. Everyone has different personalities, mindsets, and thought patterns. This applies to both you and the people who contribute to your distractions. Therefore, it will take time for you to find the approach that works best for you. The methods listed below are some methods that I have found work best for people working from home.

Keeping It Separate

The action of simply closing the door to the room of your workspace can work wonders. It will let the rest of the household know that you are busy. If a closed door does not seem to work, you can try a do not disturb sign. This will clearly indicate that you are in a meeting or in the middle of an important task.

However, if people are not your main distraction or if you don't have a door to close, you can try other barriers. You can use a curtain or screen to create separation, or you can simply cover the television screen with a sheet to avoid temptation. It's all about getting into the mindset that when you enter your workspace, you shift into work mode and leave home life aside while you work. The more you implement this separation, the easier it will become for everyone to adapt to the routine.

Switch Off Notifications

This is something that everyone should implement whether they work from home or not.

Notifications on our phones and computers interrupt us from our work. We see the little notification pop up, and even though it's a few seconds, our focus is taken away from our task. By simply turning off the notifications, we can eliminate the distraction. Some people are uncomfortable doing this in case they miss an important email or message. However, it is better to get into the habit of scheduling time into your day to check your email. You will know the best times for this depending on your work situation. If you work with someone who is known for frequent, spontaneous messages about changes to reports or sending through additional information, you can check your email a few times a day. People usually go with a morning and evening check as it helps schedule their workday, but if you need more, that's fine, as long as you have a schedule.

You can also check if your email service will allow you to disable notifications for specific senders. In this manner, you can eliminate unnecessary notifications and only allow those concerning work to filter through. Once again, these should only be addressed immediately if they are urgent. If not, they can wait until your next scheduled check-in. In terms of your phone, it is best to switch off all app notifications and only allow calls or put your phone in "Do Not

Disturb" mode. This will prevent you from constantly checking your phone or being disturbed by messages from friends and family.

Log Out of Social Media

Turning off your notifications on your social media accounts is one step to take to avoid the distractions they provide. However, you can also take it a step further and log off from your social media accounts on your device. This will make it harder for you to check your accounts as you will have to log in to do so. An extra step to access something will automatically make your brain rethink having to do so. It's not just a simple click away. If social media is your weakness when it comes to distractions, you can also opt to remove the app completely from your devices, forcing you to only use your internet browser to log in.

Take Breaks

When you're at the office, you take breaks, so you should also implement this rule when working from home. It's okay to take breaks, and this is also when you should spend some time with your family, on chores, with your pets, or checking your social media. It is even a great idea to schedule your breaks in such a way that it allows you to pick your kids up from school or for you to spend some time with them when they get home. It gives you a chance to spend time with your family and for them to also get used to a new routine.

However, just like you would at the office, you will need to return to your workspace after a specific time period. In other words, don't get carried away. Set a timer if you need a reminder, and get back to work when your break is over. In this way, you don't lose time, nor do you have to make up for it later. Your mind will also be refreshed after taking a break, and you will be able to concentrate on your work, knowing that your break was well spent.

Reward Yourself

Sometimes, you have to implement rewards to keep yourself motivated. You may think that it sounds juvenile, but it really does help your brain stay focused and increase your productivity. For example, I choose to reward myself with a cup of coffee from my favorite coffee shop if I finish a particularly difficult task. Some people may finish a report ahead of schedule and use the extra time to spend time with their family or watch an episode of their favorite show. These rewards can give you something to look forward to when you complete something and the motivation needed to avoid distractions.

Acceptance

Lastly, working from home means that you also have to accept that distractions will happen, just as they do in the office. However, being at home increases the number of distractions and temptations drastically. You are responsible for your own time, and there is no one watching you. You have to be able to manage your time efficiently to ensure that you maintain your productivity despite these distractions. It is not healthy to bury yourself in work and ignore your home life. Working from home is something that you will have to learn to balance with your home life. Thus, you cannot be too hard on yourself when you find yourself distracted. You are not failing. It is merely an opportunity to learn how you need to adapt so that distractions will happen less in the future. The sooner you accept this, the easier it will be for you to find the routine that works best for you.

Distractions while working from home is a huge learning curve for everyone. There have been countless funny stories and jokes about kids or spouses entering a workspace during an online meeting. There have even been colleagues who distract their coworkers by using filters on their Zoom calls or talking to themselves, forgetting that their mics are on! As much as we can laugh about it afterward, it can distract everyone from the meeting, and depending on your team, not everyone will find humor in the situation. Working from home doesn't have to be boring, but you must not lose sight of what is important.

If you know your kids are prone to opening the door, then lock it when you have important meetings. You can even ask a friend or family member to keep them occupied if you are a single parent or if your spouse is at work. In addition, clear communication with your partner about meeting times will minimize distractions and interruptions. This is why having a well-defined work schedule is so important. If you know when and why you cannot afford to be distracted, you can better prepare for them.

Chapter 4: Plan Ahead and Prepare a Schedule

A work schedule is an integral part of working from home. Not only is it an excellent way to stay productive and meet your deadlines, but it also helps you keep others updated. You will know exactly what meetings you have and how long you have to prepare for them. Many workers think of a schedule as being restrictive, but it is completely the opposite. A schedule will actually give you the freedom to choose your work-from-home lifestyle. If you want to ensure that you don't miss dinner with your family or that you have enough time to run some errands during the day, you can structure your schedule to accommodate this.

Scheduling is something that the most successful people do. It does not have to be incredibly detailed to be effective. For a schedule to be effective, you need to stick to it. Take former president Barack Obama, for example. His daily schedule was to wake up at 6:45 a.m., work out, read multiple newspapers, and have breakfast with his family before heading to the office at

8:50 a.m. He would then proceed to work until 10 p.m. but take a break to have dinner with his family every evening (Wiest, 2015). Most people aim to schedule their most important activities in the morning when they are most productive and leave the afternoons for checking emails, reflecting on the day's work, and making changes to upcoming schedules if need be. However, it's not the same for everyone. Some people prefer scheduling important calls and meetings in the afternoon because their mornings are filled with distractions—and that's perfectly fine, too. You know how best to structure your schedule, and that is what you should aim to do.

Why Is a Schedule Important for Working From Home?

You may feel that working from home gives you the freedom to do what you want when you want. A schedule can seem awfully boring, but it can definitely help you stay on track and be more productive. Whether we like it or not, we are creatures of habit, and our brains are accustomed to routines. This is why many people struggle with the initial shift from an office job to working from home. Every morning, you get up, get ready for work, head to the office and begin your work day. When you had to change your morning route due to traffic, how does that make you feel? Annoyed, frustrated, or super-vigilant as you drive? Your brain has stepped out of its routine and has to adapt to the change. Likewise, even though working from home may give you more time, you can only enjoy this time if you are productive during working hours. If you fail to do so, you will end up spending more time working and have fewer free hours for yourself.

A schedule can help you acquire more time for yourself in a number of ways. Firstly, it gives your brain the routine that it needs. Even the simplest of schedules will give your brain a natural rhythm that it will appreciate. Secondly, a schedule makes us more efficient with our time. If you want to be able to have dinner with your family every day, it will be a part of your schedule and therefore motivate you to finish work on time. Thirdly, it will help to develop good habits with regard to working from home. If you have a schedule that helps you follow a healthy, balanced routine, then you will be building good habits over time. It will allow you to incorporate exercise, personal time, family time, and skill-building into your day. This will not just benefit the way you work but the way you live. Lastly, a schedule will aid in eliminating bad habits and distractions from your work day. If you know that your schedule is full, you are less likely to procrastinate or be distracted.

When you know how important a schedule is and how it can benefit you, it sounds like a much better idea than just tackling each day as it comes. As much as the latter option may get you through each day, a schedule will give you peace of mind and leave you feeling less overwhelmed with on-the-spot decision-making.

Tips for Scheduling Your Day

Developing a schedule is also something that takes a bit of trial and error, as everyone has different preferences, even a few that they haven't figured out yet. For example, some people prefer working out in the morning, while others prefer to work out during lunchtime as it gives them the energy boost they need for the afternoon. You can only determine how these small changes affect your day if you try them out. In this way, you will eventually find the schedule that works best for you. I have put together some tips that I found useful when developing a schedule.

Plan the Day/Night Before

A schedule will give you a general plan for each day. However, if you take some time at the end of your workday to plan your activities for the next day, it will make a massive difference. Not only will it make the next day run smoothly, but it will also allow you to identify the tasks that will need your immediate attention and will take the most time. This will allow you to fit them into your day while maintaining the overall timing of your schedule. If you get into this routine of planning the evening before, you will find that you don't have to lose time getting organized. You will know exactly what needs to get done when you start working. This contributes to your focus and productivity levels massively.

Prioritize

Your schedule will allow you to prioritize your work in a way that will maximize your productivity. Depending on how you prefer to work, you might want to get all the big tasks of the week out of the way before tackling smaller things. However, you will also be able to schedule smaller tasks that you can finish quickly on a day when you need more personal time for your family. Try not to schedule large tasks during times when you are most likely to get distracted or interrupted. Most people have higher productivity levels in the morning. Thus, you should aim to schedule your tasks in a way that allows you to deal with important tasks first and keeps you engaged throughout the day. As you spend more time working from home, you will be able to easily recognize how your energy levels and attention span fluctuates throughout the day. This will help you prioritize your work and improve your schedule.

However, this also applies to things that you wish to prioritize in your schedule that are not work-related. For example, picking your kids up from school, having breakfast with your partner, or your daily reading time. A schedule will help you highlight your priorities and ensure that you know how to schedule your work around them.

Add Exercise to Your Schedule

When you work from home, it is very easy to forget that you need to stay active. Sitting at your computer for long hours can mean that you lose track of time or lose the motivation to exercise. This is why it is best to add it to your schedule. It then becomes an integral part of your day and will contribute to your overall well-being. This is something that many people who work from home forget about scheduling. However, if you don't add it to your schedule, you will find that you will easily push it aside for something else. Exercise is an important addition that will help boost energy levels during the day, keep you in good health, and help decrease stress levels. Thus, it is best to add it to your daily schedule and not let work push it aside. Think of it as one of your priorities that you schedule around work.

Don't Forget Your Breaks

You would not forget your breaks if you were at the office. Therefore, you should not forget to schedule your breaks when you work from home. I have known people who say they prefer not to take breaks and just continue working because they are at home. However, it is not healthy to sit at your desk for long hours. Breaks are there to remind you to move, to allow your body to get some fresh air, and to give your brain a change of pace. If you skip them, you will feel more tired at the end of the day. You will be mentally drained, your eyes will be tired, and you will have less energy for your family and pets. Taking breaks throughout the day will also allow you to get some of your household chores done, spend time with your family, and take care of your pets. Therefore, you should not forget to add breaks to your schedule because it is just as important as work.

Get Tedious Tasks Out of the Way

A schedule is an excellent way to identify and group together tedious tasks that will need your attention. You can then schedule them at a time when you can get them off your to-do list and clear your schedule for other tasks. For example, you can clear morning to get your phone calls done for the week or choose a specific time in the day to reply to all your emails. A schedule will allow you to build a routine with these tasks and prevent you from delaying them.

Use Management Tools to Help

As discussed in the second chapter, there are various management tools that can help you manage your time. This can really help your schedule by providing reminders and allowing you to sync your devices. It can be easier to organize your schedule in this manner, especially if you make a lot of changes. You can move things around accordingly without worrying about running out of space to write. In addition, I also find it useful to add information to specific tasks on my schedule. This makes it easy for me to access everything in one place, and I don't have to spend time looking for documents.

Stop Working at the End of the Workday

One of the most important tips for scheduling your day is to stop working when the workday ends. This is just as important as scheduling your tasks for the day. It will give you a clear routine for the day and give you a chance to wind down. By including a definite time to stop working, you will be more likely to stick to it and keep a healthy work schedule. There will be some times when you will need to finish up the last bit of work instead of leaving it for the next day, and that is okay. However, do not make it a habit to go beyond your work schedule.

The Ideal Work-From-Home Schedule

The ideal schedule should include all the points discussed thus far in this chapter. However, the individual times will vary depending on your start and finish times. In general, you should avoid getting up just before you are due to start working. As much as this may be tempting, this will not lead to a productive start to your day. It will take you much longer to settle down into the workday because you will spend a large part of the morning trying to wake up. To give you an idea of what a work-from-home schedule should look like, I decided to provide you with an example of my daily schedule.

Morning Alarm

You should always aim to set your alarm for a reasonable hour in the morning. For me, this is around 7:30 a.m. This gives me enough time for my morning routine before I start work at 9 a.m. However, this start time is completely up to you. Just ensure that you get at least eight hours of sleep the night before and refrain from hitting the snooze button on your alarm.

Have a Morning Routine

The first hour after waking up, I dedicate myself to my morning routine. Like many people, this consists of my morning workout, and I also listen to an audiobook or podcast. Not only does it help me start my day with a great energy boost, but I am also able to do something valuable and learn during this time. If you don't like to exercise in the morning, you can include other morning rituals like meditation, yoga, reading the newspaper, or doing some household chores to ensure that there are no distractions during the day. Whatever you choose, just ensure that you stick to it daily to build a routine.

Breakfast

At around 8:35 a.m., I enjoy my morning coffee. This is the time I spend thinking about my day ahead and what I would like to achieve, as determined by the plan I made the night before. You could use this time to have breakfast with your family or do some meal prep for the day ahead. It all depends on your personal schedule.

Start Your Workday

I begin my workday at 9 a.m. This first hour of work is when I check my emails and determine if anything needs my immediate attention. This is a great way for me to set the pace for the day ahead.

Check-Ins

At about 10:15 a.m., I determine if there are any check-ins that I need to do. This is when I will make my calls, schedule meetings for the week, and send updates. It is the time I use for human interaction before I buckle down and get into my work for the day.

Back to Work

This is the time that I block out to concentrate on my work. It varies between an hour or two depending on how long it takes me to complete my earlier check-ins. During this time, I try to avoid distractions by putting my phone away and focusing on the tasks that I have scheduled.

Hydration Reminder

Working from home can definitely make you lose track of time. Reminders to drink water and stay hydrated are actually a great way to take small pauses throughout the day. I like to put one in the morning around 11:30 a.m. because I know I tend to get caught up in my work. We often forget how important it is to stay hydrated, and cups of coffee will not do the job.

Lunch Break

My lunch break is usually at 12:30 p.m. This is when I will step away from my desk for about 45 minutes. I will either prepare my own lunch or take a quick walk to the deli nearby. This gives me a much-needed break and allows me to reset for the afternoon.

Afternoon Routine

When I get back to work in the afternoon, I get back into my workspace and dive back into my afternoon schedule. If I find my energy ebbing, I sometimes take my laptop and sit in a different spot. I know this is not an option for everyone, but simply having a slightly different location can make you perk up.

Human Interactions

Around 2:30 p.m., I check in with a colleague or two who also work from home. This gives me time to still experience a bit of socializing even though I'm not in the office. It's also good to connect with colleagues who battle with isolation when working from home.

Break

I then take another short break around 3 p.m. to get some fresh air. Those who don't like exercising in the morning could also schedule their workout for around this time. This time really helps with the afternoon slump that many workers experience.

Reflection

After my afternoon break, I use the time to reflect on the day's work and ensure that everything in my workspace is in order for the next day. This does not take up much time but will help you start the next day with ease.

Planning

The time after my afternoon reflection is used to plan my tasks for the next day. This is around 5 p.m., and I go over my schedule and insert anything that needs to be added. I also check my weekly targets to ensure that I am on track to meet my productivity goals.

End of Day

At 6:30 p.m., I switch off my computer and step away from my workspace. This gives me the physical and mental separation that I need to end my workday and enjoy my personal time.

Your schedule does not have to have similar timings to work. It just needs to follow a routine that works for you. Always keep in mind that a schedule can be as detailed or brief as you want. It just has to provide the structure and routine that your brain needs to maintain productivity and the essential time management needed to meet your personal and professional goals.

Email Management

Going through emails and replying to them can take up a lot of time. They can also turn into a distraction when notifications take you away from what you are working on. This is why it is wise to manage your emails before they overwhelm you. Here are some tips for email management that will save you time and improve your time management.

Create Email Checkpoints

Email notifications act as distractions. It is best to turn them off and create email checkpoints in your workday. Some people only check their emails once a day. However, implementing a morning and afternoon check is good practice. It will help you identify what needs your immediate attention in the mornings and if you need to add anything to your schedule. Depending on the type of work you do, you may need more checkpoints throughout your day. Although, you should never spend too much time on them and only go through what is important, ignoring newsletters and advertisements.

Quick Replies Come First

When checking your email, you will find that there are emails you can reply to quickly and some that need a bit more time to address. Those that can be quickly dealt with come first. You can reply to them immediately and get them off your to-do list. Those that require more time should be assigned a due date and added to your schedule accordingly.

Organize Your Mailbox

It's nearly impossible to have a mailbox with no saved messages. Sometimes we need to recall conversations and find information. Therefore, as good practice, you should organize your mailbox. You can use folders and assign each email to relevant folders. This keeps your mailbox tidy, and you can easily locate your emails according to your filing system.

Use Filters

Filters can be useful to automatically separate and organize your email. This is extremely useful if you subscribe to newsletters or receive automated messages from your company. You can change the settings on your email so that these can get filed into the relevant folder automatically by recognizing the email address. That way, you can deal with them when you have time because they are not directly related to your work.

Implement a Time Limit

When you are checking your email, implement a time limit so that you don't spend too much time on them. You should aim to quickly scan the list of emails and identify those which are most important. Go through those first before moving on to the others. In this manner, if you reach your time limit, you know that you did not miss any of the urgent emails requiring your attention. The others can be dealt with at the next checkpoint.

These simple steps will help you manage your email and time more effectively. You don't have to worry about half of your day disappearing while responding to emails.

Exercise: Create Your own Schedule

Now that you know why a schedule is so important and how to go about structuring one, you should go ahead and create your own. Use the example provided with my own schedule and see how it can be adapted for your workday. It will take a few tries to perfect it, but it will never be set in stone. You will find yourself making changes as your priorities change and as you settle into your work-from-home lifestyle.

In addition, your schedule should also aim to address your weekly, monthly, and quarterly goals. Every task you complete will contribute to your overall goals. This will help you keep track of your productivity, ensure that your deadlines are met and that you are managing your time well. In the next chapter, we will discuss the importance of setting goals and the role they play in effective time management.

Chapter 5: Setting Goals and Staying Motivated

The longer you work from home, you will find that staying motivated can become more difficult. This is because you have to do it yourself. There's no one with you, encouraging you, providing guidance, or the occasional pep talk. Sure, you can reach out to a colleague, but not everyone has someone to talk to when motivation levels drop. This is one of the reasons why it is important to set goals. They help you stay motivated by providing achievable targets. This makes an incredible difference to how you will perceive your work. I know this for a fact, as setting goals played a huge part in helping me improve my time management and increase my productivity while working from home.

Likewise, dressing for work can also help you stay motivated by provoking a sense of confidence or comfort. Even though no one from the office can see the clothes you wear, they will be able to sense your mood and be inspired by your attitude. It's a classic case of "fake it until you make it." You dress the part, and your brain will eventually begin to feel like joining the party. It's important to note that dressing the part means different things to different people—but we'll go through that in a bit. First, let's look at how setting goals can benefit your work-from-home lifestyle.

The Benefits of Setting Goals

When you lack motivation, it can be difficult to work. You will find yourself being less productive, and you will be easily tempted by distractions. Simply put, if there's no motivation, you're not going to want to get anything done. However, by planning, having a schedule, and setting goals, you will have something to work towards. This simple act keeps you in control of your time and helps you track your productivity. It also keeps you in the right frame of mind by always reminding you what you are working towards. I will take you through some of the benefits of setting goals before we go through how you can create goals for yourself.

Increased Productivity

Setting goals can help increase your productivity by providing accountability, motivation, and pride. How? Well, firstly, if you define your goals, you are accountable for meeting them. No matter the size, or whether they are a company or personal goals, having accountability for them is important. You know that meeting these targets allows you to contribute to the bigger picture and ensures that you grow personally and professionally. Secondly, each time you achieve a goal, you are motivated to move on to the next one. That sense of achievement is one that we would like to have with us at all times. Thus, we carry on working towards our goals to keep chasing that high. Also, I don't know about you, but when I put a due date on something, it's like the time estimate that the GPS gives you for reaching your destination. My competitive nature makes me want to beat it!

Lastly, achieving your goals gives you a sense of pride. You can track your progress and even evaluate how much you have grown in your career. This is why companies like you to set goals that can be evaluated during performance reviews. They can track if you're meeting requirements, reaching targets, and achieving your overall goals. Over time, you will continue to improve, and, in turn, this will spur you on, resulting in increased focus and productivity. The best part is that you have total control over this process. You know what you are capable of, so you can set your targets accordingly and occasionally push yourself to test your capabilities. In this manner, you never stay at the same level but continue to improve.

Creativity and Innovation

When you have goals to meet, you will automatically find yourself innovating and thinking creatively to meet them. This is especially true for those working from home. When you have a schedule that clearly shows how much time you have dedicated to a specific project, you will find ways to refine the way you work. It could mean using your management tools efficiently to save you time or prioritizing your work in such a way that your goals are achieved on time.

Personally, I like to set daily, weekly, monthly, and annual goals. This may seem like a lot, but it helps me stay on track and maintain my productivity levels. However, this does not mean that I don't have slow-paced days. Instead, having these goals broken down into small targets allows me to schedule my day accordingly. Thus, if I am having a day when my energy or motivation levels are low, I can do the lighter tasks associated with a specific project goal. This still positively contributes to my productivity, and I don't feel like I have wasted time. Therefore, I am still able to accomplish my goals on these days, and it gives me a bit more motivation for the next day.

This type of adaptation to the way you think and work towards your goal will occur the more you get to know yourself and the way you work from home. Everyone will experience highs and lows, but the key is to keep moving. Small steps are better than none.

Fewer Missed Workdays

Missed workdays are a common occurrence in offices where motivation levels among employees are low. The same happens when motivation is low, and you are working from home. If employees start working slower because they are unmotivated and bored, they will start questioning whether they need to go to work at all. In fact, the 2019 Mind the Workplace report by Mental Health America reported that 58% of employees lack motivation. This impacts mental health and results in missed workdays. It can also impact your physical health as stress often manifests as physical ailments.

By setting small, achievable goals, you can work on improving your motivation at work. If you find that the work is not challenging enough, you set your own challenges. You have to be your own cheerleader, motivating yourself to do better. If you keep yourself engaged in this manner, chances are you won't miss work because of the lack of motivation.

Improved Skills

As with anything in life, practice makes you perfect. Likewise, setting goals will help you improve your skills over time. As you meet your targets, you can see how much you have improved. For example, maybe when you started working from home, quarterly reports took you two weeks to complete by the time you got the relevant information from your colleagues and compiled the report. However, six months later, you were able to halve that time by using effective management tools, and in a year, you streamlined the process further and got it down to a few days. Goals can help you achieve this by keeping your targets in sight. They give you a clear view of the larger picture while providing motivation through the small steps.

You will get better time management skills, learn how best to improve your productivity, and how to better keep motivation levels high. These are skills you can also pass on to others in your team.

Rewards

If you are working from home, you can reward yourself for achieving your goals which help to increase motivation. The bigger the goal achieved, the larger the reward. For example, if you manage to achieve your goals for the day, maybe you can reward yourself with a trip to your favorite coffee shop or finish work early to spend time with your family. Even the smallest of rewards, like giving yourself 15 minutes of internet time when you finish a report, can make all the difference. You are giving yourself something in return for achieving a goal. It's a dopamine hit that your brain will remember and crave more of because it improves your mood. Thus, it will motivate you to achieve the next goal so that you can experience a reward again.

How to Develop Measurable Goals

Now that you understand why goals are so important in keeping you motivated, let's go through some steps that will help you develop measurable goals for working at home.

1. Identify Your Goals

The first thing you need to do is take the time to define your goals. If you are a remote team member, try to align these goals with that of your company. In this way, you can track how you are contributing to your company's goals, which is great for your annual performance review. If you are a freelancer, you want to define your goals in a similar way, but instead of company goals, you will have your end goals as a professional. What do you want to achieve? I wanted to have the freedom to travel while I worked, and I achieved that by setting goals to improve my time management and increase my productivity. Now, I can spend a few hours working and spend the rest of my day enjoying the country I am in while still hitting my daily targets.

Your goals should reflect the growth you wish to achieve in your career and life as a whole. It's like the infamous question recruiters ask in interviews, "Where do you see yourself in five years?". Be specific with your goals, and ensure that they are measurable. This will allow you to easily track your progress.

2. Break Down Goals Into Smaller Tasks

Once you have your measurable goals, it's time to start breaking them down into smaller tasks. A good way to do this is to think of all the components that you will need to have to achieve the goal. Then from those components, start identifying the individual tasks that make it up. Think of each goal as a book you have to write. You need to outline the chapters and then break down those chapters into sections and subsections if need be. In this manner, you will clearly identify the tasks you have to complete before you can achieve your goal.

3. Schedule Accordingly

The third step is to take these tasks and fit them into your schedule. You will need to allocate time to each task and have a due date. There is no one who better understands your work schedule and how you work than you. Therefore, you will know how much time each task needs for completion. However, you also need to afford yourself a buffer. This is extra time just in case of any delays that may occur in a project. Over time you will get a better estimate of how big this buffer must be, but I would suggest starting with a week.

These schedules are a great reminder for important dates, milestones and for tracking productivity. You can use them for yourself and for your team.

4. Review and Adapt as Necessary

The last step is to always remember that these goals and smaller tasks will change over time. You will need to regularly review and adapt them to ensure that they still align with your larger goals. Maybe you will need to make changes to the schedule because you noticed you are working faster or slower than expected. Your goal could have even changed due to circumstances in your personal life, like moving house or having a child. You just have to ensure that your goals are always relevant and you know what has to be done to achieve them.

SMART Goals

I'm sure you would have heard the term SMART goals before. Companies love throwing this acronym around when assessing employees' performance or discussing the key performance indicators (KPIs) when describing a role. SMART goals were first described in 1981 by George Doran. They are still an excellent way to set goals and evaluate personal performance and productivity. This is why companies love them. They have measurable goals that you are accountable for and that they can easily evaluate. By setting these up for yourself, the same thing will happen. Instead of just having your goals in your head, you are putting them down and giving yourself a tangible target.

The acronym serves as a reminder to develop goals that are:

Specific—Your goals must always be specific. To ensure that they are, you need to answer five questions. What, why, who, when, and where? If you answer these for each goal, you will get the specific details that need to be addressed.

Measurable—Goals have to be measurable. This means that you should be able to easily track these goals by the milestones in place. For example, a specific number of articles completed, sales made, or recruitments. There need to be numbers that you can assess.

Achievable—Your goals also have to be realistic. Yes, they should have an element of challenge so that you can reach new heights, but they should still be achievable. Think of it this way, you're setting goals, not creating a wish list. If you achieve your goal, then you can aim for more.

Relevant—This is somewhat linked to your goals being achievable. You also want them to be relevant to the work you are doing. Thus, you should always check that it fits into your priorities.

Time-Bound—You need to give your goals a deadline. There's no use setting a measurable goal if you don't have a deadline associated with it. That just makes it easy for you to keep pushing it aside. Even long-term goals need a deadline so that you remain motivated to work toward them.

By establishing SMART goals, you are establishing the targets that you are holding yourself accountable for. You can share them with others if you want to ensure that someone checks in with you occasionally to see if you are meeting them. I also like to keep my goals document somewhere where it is easily accessible so that I can check if I am meeting my goals.

Dress the Part

One of the things that people love about working from home is not having to dress for work every day. It is a relief not having to think about what to wear every morning or even ironing your clothes, for that matter. However, over time you will find that this will also impact your motivation levels. This is why it is important that you also establish your own dress code for work. When you are dressed for work, your mind automatically shifts into gear and gets ready for the day. It also introduces a sense of routine and normalcy to your day. In addition, when you dress for work, it also makes you feel better about yourself. As with most occasions, if we look good, we feel good.

This doesn't mean that you have to dress like you would in the office. You can establish your own work-from-home dress style. It just means that you shouldn't be wearing your pajamas or sweatpants all day. You need a clear separation between home and work life, and this includes your clothes. Even though no one else can see what you are wearing, you know, and that makes all the difference. It's like when we get home from the office, we tend to kick off our shoes, lose the tie, or maybe even change into something more comfortable. We have learned to associate those clothes with comfort, relaxation, and even sleep. If you then wear these for work, you will not be motivated to work because your body will be in relaxation mode. This is how dressing differently for work will help you stay motivated and focused.

How to Plan Your Work Wardrobe

We all have different styles and different levels of comfort, and some may even have work dress codes to consider even when working from home. In addition, some people have to attend a lot of online meetings while others have minimal contact with other people during the day. Therefore, there should be some thought that goes into your workwear. However, once you decide on your style, you will find that you will save a lot of time in deciding what to wear and will also be less frazzled when an unexpected online meeting occurs.

Here are some points to consider when choosing your work attire:

It Saves Time

Having clothes that are set aside for work saves time in two ways. Firstly, you don't have to go through your entire wardrobe every morning trying to figure out what to wear. It is almost as if you have a work uniform and eliminates indecisiveness. Secondly, if you have an important meeting during the day, you don't have to waste time changing your clothes just for the meeting. You may think that the time saved is minimal, but it really does make a difference.

Strike a Balance Between Comfort and Style

Some companies have dress codes, while others remain casual. The trick when working from home is to strike a balance between comfort and style. You should aim for smart casual clothes that still offer a bit of comfort but still make you feel confident. You need to look at yourself and feel as if you could go to the office with the clothes you have on and not stand out too much.

This balance also doesn't mean business up top where the camera ends. That was one of the biggest work-from-home jokes during the pandemic. Men with dress shirts, ties, and then their boxers. Or women with dressy blouses and pajama bottoms. If you've ever done this, have you noticed how your demeanor changes immediately after the meeting? Your body slouches, and you lose all your energy and motivation. This is because the act of being half-dressed makes you feel as if you are acting as someone who is working and not as if you are actually working. Thus, you should always commit to your work clothes fully.

Opt for Neutrals on Meeting Days

This is not a hard and fast rule, but it is best to wear neutral colors when you know you're going to have meetings. Prints can be distracting to others, and neutral colors or monotones will appear more professional no matter what you are wearing.

Choose Clothes That Make You Feel Confident

We all have an outfit or two that gives us confidence. Don't hesitate to wear them if you are at home. There will be days when you need an extra pick-me-up, and these outfits will make a difference. It will immediately make you feel confident and give you the boost you need to get through the day.

Be Quirky but Presentable

Working from home also allows you to dress according to your personality. It's great to bring your quirkiness into your clothes and inject some creative energy into your work. When people are allowed to express themselves through the way they dress, they are more likely to work better because they feel more comfortable. However, this does not apply to every industry. Thus, people who have to dress formally in the office can opt for a more casual style at home if they find it more motivating and less stifling. Just try to remember that you still have to be presentable when attending meetings.

No matter what clothes you choose, just be consistent in getting dressed every day. You need to be able to look in the mirror, feel like you're going to work and be happy about the way you look. The more time you spend working from home, the better you will get at defining your style. Some people prefer to include activewear in their work clothes because they know they will have to hit the gym at some point during the day or have to do some work around the house. The choice is ultimately yours but just ensure that you have work clothes that are distinct from your home clothes.

Setting goals and having a work wardrobe are two very important elements of keeping yourself motivated when you work from home. They will also fluctuate in their efficacy, but you will learn how to identify what works best for you. The entire process of working from home will teach you more about yourself as a worker. You will learn what motivates you, what drains you, and how you need to structure your time to ensure maximum productivity. Knowing your strengths and weaknesses is what we will discuss next.

Chapter 6: Know Your Forte

All employees, whether they work in an office, at home, or are self-employed, tend to focus on their weaknesses and not their strengths. In an attempt to improve ourselves, we make the common mistake of focusing on eliminating our weaknesses. After all, eliminating weaknesses will make us stronger employees overall. Our weaknesses are also what our employers generally point out and tell us that we need to work on. However, a strengths-based approach is a much better way to achieve success at work (Aguinis et al., 2012). If we shift our focus to our strengths, we are able to work on them and solidify our approach to our work. We are able to approach the work feeling motivated and enthusiastic because we know it is what we are good at. In contrast, when faced with our weaknesses, we tend to doubt ourselves every step of the way.

The other thing about a strengths-based approach is that it helps you manage your time better. I discovered this early on when I started working from home—although, at the time, I hadn't really identified it for what it was. It became pretty evident that I enjoyed getting the easier things done before I tackled something I found difficult. However, what I was actually doing was using my strengths to complete the tasks I knew I was good at. This allowed me to clear my to-do list and give myself ample time to work on a task that was not my forte. In this way, I didn't have to worry about running out of time to meet all my deadlines. If I had focused on the hard task first, I may have fallen behind or rushed through my other work just to meet the deadline and not worry about quality. Having this knowledge also has other benefits, which I will go through next.

Why It's Good to Know Your Strengths

Knowing your strengths will help you perform better in all areas of your life. It allows you to do things confidently, knowing that the results will be positive. More specifically, it boosts productivity and results in you being more engaged in your work. It helps to shift your mind to positive outcomes and a more meaningful work experience. Let's analyze this a bit further.

Increases Productivity

When you know your strengths, you will be more productive in your work. This is because these strengths will allow you to proceed with confidence. When you have this attitude toward your work, you will be excited, motivated, energized, and focused. These automatically give your productivity a boost as you won't waste time doubting or second-guessing yourself.

Boosts Self-Confidence

Knowing your strengths definitely boosts self-confidence. You are more aware of what you can do and will not shy away from it. It will also help you see yourself differently and look at things from a different perspective. You will be able to better assess situations, your abilities, and the way you handle different tasks. To put it simply, you know what you bring to the table. This self-awareness makes an incredible difference when structuring your schedule and managing your time. It also helps you to identify strengths in others as well. This is because your mindset has shifted regarding strengths and weaknesses.

Improves the Way You Engage With Your Work

When you know that you're working on something you're good at, your attitude toward your work changes. The fact that you can work knowing that you have the right skills for the job allows you to engage with your work differently. You will feel positive while working and motivated to continue. Even when the task is challenging, you will see it as a way to improve your strength, much the same way a weightlifter always pushes their limits. Working in this way means that you are constantly improving and getting better at what you do. In fact, according to a study done by Gallup, employees that use their strengths daily are six times more likely to be engaged on the job (Sorenson, 2014).

Increased Retention Among Team Members

Being able to identify your strengths and those of others on your team is a great way to also keep your team members happy and engaged in their work. This can make a huge difference to your team's productivity as a whole. You will also find that team members are more likely to stay in their positions and not leave because they are frustrated or overwhelmed with trying to improve their weaknesses. They will feel more appreciated when their strengths are recognized. The team will run smoothly, with everyone knowing what they can best handle. Therefore, no time has to be spent on recruiting and training new team members.

When you know your strengths, you will understand yourself better. It will help you identify things like why certain tasks drain your energy or why you have a tendency to help others. This knowledge is powerful when you work from home and are accountable for your time and work.

How to Identify Your Work

Strengths

We often don't notice our true strengths because we have not yet identified and named them. They are considered a part of our personality and are not recognized. By taking the time to identify your strengths, you can understand yourself better and be able to approach your work with this newfound insight. Although, how do you go about identifying your strengths if you haven't quite figured them out yet?

Ask Others

The first place to start if you have no idea of your strengths is to ask the people around you. They will have noticed things that you would probably take for granted or have misidentified. For example, you may be introverted by nature and don't often speak during meetings, which you might have identified as a weakness. However, maybe your colleagues have noticed that you are a good listener and observant, leading to you bringing up good points when you do speak. This is a valuable strength that you probably missed because you focus on your weakness instead.

Obviously, this may be harder to do if you work from home exclusively and don't really share facetime with others. In these instances, you should take notice when people compliment you about the things you do at work. If you make a note of these situations, it may help you identify what skills you used and where your strengths lie. In this way, you can then identify how you could best utilize these skills more in your daily tasks.

Think About What You Enjoy Doing

Take some time to think about what you enjoy doing at work and in your personal time. What is it about that activity that you enjoy? Maybe you like to write or draw because you enjoy immersing yourself in the intricacies of the activity. This could mean that you have excellent attention to detail and a creative way of thinking. In turn, it might explain why you like working on the company newsletter or enjoy when you have to liaise with the marketing team.

Trying to link what you enjoy doing to the trait you exhibit will give you a whole new perspective on yourself and your strengths. You will learn more about yourself and also shift your thinking. The next time you enjoy a task, you may even discover a new strength that you didn't even realize you had developed. It all comes from understanding yourself better.

Relationship Style

At work, we tend to have a specific relationship style that we prefer. You should pay attention to the relationships that you find inspiring and energizing. These are the relationships that will indicate your strengths. The work relationships that you tend to avoid or have a hard time working with will also give you clues about your strengths. This can come in handy when you have to navigate working with others. You will know exactly who you will work well with and why.

When Are You in the Zone?

You know those moments at work when you lose track of time because you're so focused on what you're working on? That's your flow state or when you're in the zone. The task you're working on doesn't drain your energy, and you feel fully engaged and excited about what you are doing. Identifying these moments and what you're working on will tell you about your strengths. This is how you want to feel whenever you work on something, as it leads to you being more productive.

Pay Attention When You Ask for Help

Those instances when you feel like you're in over your head and you need help can also enable you to identify your strengths, too. These will be tasks that will most likely leave you feeling unmotivated and drained. However, this can still indicate that your strength comes from knowing yourself and what you are capable of. You know when to ask for help, and you could also know whom to ask. This would indicate that you are aware of the strengths of others.

Name Your Strengths

Once you have done these exercises, you can actually sit down and look at the strengths that you have identified. It is worthwhile naming these strengths in a way that makes them stand out. For example, instead of saying you are a people person, you could say that your strength is that you're an effective communicator. This highlights your strength and gives you confidence in your word choice.

Take a Test

Another way to identify your strengths is to take an online test. There are various tests that are offered by credible sources that will help you identify your strengths, personality type, and which career you are suited for. The Myers-Briggs personality test is one of the most popular tests available and one that people like doing to learn more about themselves (NERIS Analytics Limited, 2022). However, you should always remember that your personality type will not always correlate with your work personality. It will give you great insight into yourself, though, and help you understand some things a bit better when it comes to how you make decisions and react to certain situations.

Career tests are also useful in the same manner. Although, you shouldn't quit your job because the test doesn't match your current career. Instead, you should assess the information it gives you. This will tell you your strengths, and you can figure out how to use them in your current job.

As I said before, working from home will teach you a lot about yourself and your approach to work. Identifying your strengths will enable you to better achieve each of the previous steps we have gone through regarding time management. You will be able to determine what kind of workspace you need when you can work without distraction, how to schedule according to your strengths, and how to set goals to improve these strengths over time. Every aspect of time management when working from home feeds into each other. This is how you will learn to adapt and grow, maintain your productivity, and live the healthy balanced life that everyone craves.

The last chapter will discuss the sixth and final step for effective time management at home, which is learning to unplug.

Chapter 7: Unplug and Switch Off

Time management when working from home also includes when you unplug and switch off for the day. This aspect is more important than many realize and should not be ignored. Not only does scheduling the end of your workday give you a definite time to switch off, but it also provides a routine to your day. Without having a clear end to the day, your home life and work life will never be separated. We live in a world where this separation is hard to achieve, no matter which industry you are in. Many people leave the office at the end of the day but will still respond to work emails and messages when they see them at home. This small act actually eliminates any work/life balance you seek to achieve. The more you respond to work after working hours, the more it begins to feel like a normal activity to you. In turn, because people know you will respond, they will continue sending you things even though they know you are at home. This is further exacerbated when you work from home and have team members in different countries. If your working hours are not clearly stated, you will be continuously bombarded with emails, requests, and messages.

In order to maintain a work/life balance, your schedule needs to have a clear end of the day. It doesn't have to be the same time every day, but you need to step away from your workspace and switch off your devices. Your time management practices will allow you the time to come up with a plan of action for the next day, and it will also give you time to address your email in the morning. In this way, everything that needs to be addressed will be. There is no need for anyone to contact you in your personal time. Likewise, there is no need for you to continue working after your working day ends. You can be confident that everything will be handled as your schedule already includes these actions at the appropriate times.

So, if you have already implemented the previous steps of time management, you should not have any issues with stepping away from your computer. If you still battle to unplug, don't worry. You're not alone. Even I battled to unplug and switch off when I first started working from home. It's so easy to just keep working, and I used to rationalize it by thinking I'd still be on the way home if I was working at the office. However, the extended work hours only resulted in higher productivity for a very short while. After that, it actually had a negative impact. This is why it's important that you know why you should unplug and how you can achieve a healthy work/life balance when your work and home life share the same space.

Why Unplug?

Unplugging from technology is critical for our health. It's not only about working, the amount of screen time we accumulate in a day is shocking. This constant state of being plugged into our devices leads us to forget that there are other ways to relax. Working from home can sometimes complicate things because we find reasons to plug in. I've heard every reason why it's okay to stay plugged in when working from home. People feel like they need to make up for the time they lost during the day, they are used to getting home later from the office, or they think they can just work in front of the television after hours. However, these are all the wrong ways of thinking and often mean that you do not have an effective schedule in place. Once you have a schedule, your time management will automatically get better, and there will be no reason to work after hours. Unplugging from technology and work is possible—and the reasons to unplug far outweigh why you think you need to stay plugged in.

Unplugging Helps You Stop Working

The simple act of shutting down your computer helps you step away from your workspace and enter personal time. If you cannot step away from your phone, it is best to turn off email notifications after work. In this manner, you establish a clear boundary between work and home. If you work with different team members or have a manager that often contacts you after working hours, you may want to inform them clearly of your working hours. You can even activate an automatic reply before you log off for the day, reassuring people that you will reply when you are back online.

The more you implement these actions, the more people will understand that you are unavailable outside of working hours. They will either start contacting you before you log out for the day or will know that they will receive a response later. If you are self-employed, unplugging will help you establish healthy boundaries and prevent you from becoming consumed by work. It's easy to forget that you need to stop if you live alone, but if you don't unplug, it will lead to negative feelings about work that will affect your overall productivity and performance.

It Benefits Your Mental Health

No matter your age, profession, or schedule, it is easy to develop an unhealthy relationship with technology. It has so effortlessly blended into our lives that being unplugged can even invoke a fear of missing out. It's not just the computer that has this effect on us either. Our phones, smart watches, tablets, and other devices ensure that we are constantly plugged in. Every alert and notification can pull us into an unhealthy spiral.

Notifications from work can leave you feeling anxious about what awaits you or can even make you abandon your personal time to deal with them. Social media interactions also don't always have a positive influence on our mental health. It can leave us feeling unhappy and envious of others. These feelings easily affect us and make us feel as if we're not doing enough or accomplishing enough in our own lives. As a result, we may start letting that influence the way we work and live in an attempt to match what we see online. This is never a good idea as what is posted on social media rarely reflects real life. In addition, trying to be something that you're not, takes away from your happiness and will leave you feeling disconnected from yourself.

This is why it is best to unplug for the sake of your mental health. You do not have to be the perfect employee, friend, or family member that is available 24/7 and replying to everything that you see online. Try to remember that it is best to be mindful of the present. Unplug at the end of the day and focus on giving yourself the attention that would otherwise be taken up by unimportant things online.

Improves Relationships

Unplugging from your devices at the end of the day can greatly improve your relationships with the people around you. Your family and friends also deserve your time and attention. Can you imagine how frustrating it would be if you kept walking away from the dinner table to respond to work messages? Those dearest to you would feel unimportant because your work is taking priority over spending time with them. In addition, when you work from home, you often need their support during working hours. You will probably tell them when you have important meetings or ask them to respect your working hours and not disturb you until you take a break. Not being able to have the same mindset when it comes to the people who matter the most to you is just not right.

Being able to unplug from work and technology, in general, will help you build and experience more meaningful relationships with those around you. You will be able to give them your full attention and focus on the moments being shared instead of sharing those moments with an unclear mind. This is when you can really attain the work/life balance that you desire.

It Helps You Sleep Better

If you battle to sleep at night, most people will tell you to develop a nightly routine that does not include technology. This is because the blue light from computer and phone screens will prevent you from falling asleep. Also, if you work way beyond your working hours, you will be left feeling tired but anxious. This anxiety can prevent you from getting a good night's sleep.

This is what many people who work from home fail to realize. If you spend more time working, you leave less time for home life. Then, in an attempt to make up for it, you sleep less and wake up feeling tired and unable to have a good start to your day. Thus, working longer hours actually takes away from your productivity instead of contributing to it.

It Helps You Be More Productive During Work Hours

Being able to unplug and leave your workspace in the evening plays a crucial role in your productivity during working hours. It is a shift in thinking that will power you through your day. Firstly, when you have a schedule that includes your tasks for the day and a time that your day will end, you have a clear plan as to what needs to get done. This gives you the motivation to focus on your work because you want to ensure that you finish your tasks for the day.

Secondly, unplugging at the end of the day gives you the time you need to decompress, relax and spend time doing the things that make you happy. This makes a difference in how your day ends and the state of mind with which you go to bed. You will be able to sleep better and wake up refreshed and ready to take on the day with a clear mind. There will be a decrease in feelings of resentment towards work, and your energy levels will be higher.

Unplugging at the end of the day when working from home is a necessity. There will be days when the time at which you unplug will change due to your schedule, and that's okay. You just have to ensure that you do. Working long, extended hours just because you are working from home will actually lead to you being less productive. It also increases the chances of you suffering from anxiety, stress, and even burnout.

There is no reason for you to work long hours if you maintain a work schedule. Even when longer hours equal more money, you have to question if it is worth what you are losing. You will have poorer health, your relationships will be strained, and you could be missing out on some very important moments that you will never get back. I didn't have a plan when I started working from home, I just knew that I had to make it work. This led to me working insane hours just because I was at home and I could. However, I quickly noticed that the initial benefits I had experienced with working from home diminished over time. I was back to being tired all the time and had little energy for activities or people outside of work. This is when I realized that I needed to learn how to unplug for the day.

How to Switch off at the End of the Day

Much like learning how to plan your schedule when working from home, learning how to switch off at the end of the day takes practice. The actual act of switching off your devices may not necessarily be difficult. However, shifting your mind away from work in the evenings is where the difficulty lies. This is because even though you're not in front of your computer, your mind will still be thinking of what you should and could do. When this happens, you don't give yourself time to relax, and you take away from the time spent with your loved ones because you are not fully present in the moment.

You, therefore, have to spend time trying to figure out the best way to get out of the work zone physically and mentally. Here are some tips that can help you switch off from work at the end of the day.

Develop Clear Boundaries

Clear boundaries are often something we forget about at work. We may have them in our personal relationships, but with regard to work, it seems like we don't have the opportunity or right to have them. However, work is one of the most crucial situations where we should establish clear boundaries. This is especially true when you work from home. You need to develop clear boundaries with your colleagues and with yourself. I know this is easier said than done—but trust me, it will improve your life drastically.

The first step is to set a boundary for yourself. This will entail determining your ideal working hours at home. Everyone will have slightly different availability depending on schedules, time differences between remote workers, company policy, and home responsibilities. You will have to determine the timing that best meets your requirements. Once you have this in place, you can let the people you work with know that you will be unavailable outside these hours. Of course, there will be certain situations when emergencies occur, or you have to work longer hours to meet a deadline. However, they will be few and far between, and people need to know this. You can even set up automatic replies to emails outside of working hours, so people know you will respond when you are back at work.

Weekends, vacations, and even personal time off should have the same clear boundaries. The more you enforce them, the more your brain will be at ease with leaving work behind at the end of the day.

Move Away From Your Workspace

To reinforce the boundaries you create, it is good to move away from your workspace outside of working hours. This puts some distance between you and your devices. If it is possible, you should also have separate devices for work and personal use. In this way, you won't be pulled back into work if you are likely to receive notifications. You have to realize that moving away from your workspace means leaving the office for the day. This is why unplugging or logging off is so important. If you don't switch your devices off, you might see or even hear a notification that will draw you back. Physical separation from your workspace can help you avoid this.

Have a Shutdown Ritual

Remember how we said our brains like routines? Having a clear shutdown ritual will provide this. It will help you separate work from your home life even though you are in the same place. Your schedule should already contribute to your shutdown ritual by preparing your mind. It does this by letting you reflect on the work done and what needs to be done the next day. You need to extend this into a daily ritual. When you work from the office, you have a clear ritual at the end of the day. You switch off your computer, pack your things away and then make your way home. In a similar fashion, you need to develop a ritual like this when you work from home.

Since there's no commute, you can instead ensure that your workspace is clear of clutter, your devices have been switched off, and use your commute time for another activity. If you get into the habit of doing this every day, it becomes second nature to you, and a clear routine will be developed.

Choose a Hobby

If you choose a hobby to indulge in post-work, you can utilize your previous commute time. This will further contribute to your shutdown ritual. In addition, you will be able to dedicate time to something that you've always wanted to do. For example, you can take up painting, boxing, or even gardening. These are also excellent activities to decompress after a work day and deal with a bad mood before spending time with your family and friends. Therefore, a hobby will not only allow you to switch off from work but contribute to your physical and mental health as well.

Run Errands

Using the time after you switch off from work to run errands creates the physical separation you need from your workspace. It can be a part of your shutdown ritual every day and will help occupy your mind with something other than work. I know it's unlikely that you will have an errand to run every day, but you can also alternate it with your hobby. In this manner, you won't get too bored with your routine. The main aspect is to step away from your workspace and provide your mind with a distraction.

Decrease Screen Time

The concept of a technology detox has become quite popular in recent years. Technology has definitely made our lives easier, but it also takes up a precious amount of time. Many people often find it surprising just how much screen time they accumulate daily—even if it is work-related. Thus, you can practice decreasing your screen time in the evenings by switching off your devices completely. Instead of losing time by scrolling through social media, use this time to spend with your family, call a friend, or even dedicate yourself to reading. This can make the time meaningful and constructive.

Decreasing screen time in the evenings can also help you sleep better. Excessive blue light is known to decrease melatonin levels and prevent sleep at night (Chai, 2021). Natural blue light from the sun plays an important role in our daily routines by keeping us awake during the day. However, artificial blue light prevents the natural progression in our brains toward preparing our bodies for rest. Thus, decreasing screen time after work is a great way to switch off from work and relax.

Choose to Be Mindful

Mindfulness is something that everyone struggles with nowadays. How can we be mindful of the present when there are so many other things to worry about? This is one of the downfalls of modern life. However, choosing to be mindful doesn't necessarily mean shutting everything out and focusing on a singular activity. It means choosing to recognize when these overbearing thoughts enter your mind and taking steps to pay attention in spite of them.

In terms of switching off for the day, choosing to be mindful will help put work aside and focus on the aspects of home life. It will mean recognizing when you get anxious thinking about the work you still have to do and consciously choosing to accept that it will be handled when you get back to work. Likewise, it will enable you to recognize that you are missing out on important moments of home life by worrying about something else. By being mindful of your thoughts, you can work toward achieving a balance between your work and home life over time.

Engage With Friends and Family

Spending time with friends, family, and even pets is an excellent way to switch off from work. When you do something enjoyable and strengthen the bonds with those closest to you, it will help you leave work behind for the day. You can use the time after work to take your kids to practice, hang out with friends, have a date night with your partner, or even take your dogs for a walk. These activities can be rotated during the week, depending on everyone's schedules.

The time you spend with others is important for your mental health and for maintaining relationships. You will have the time to enjoy moments you would otherwise miss out on because of work. This has really helped me while working from home. I got to see what I was missing out on when I was working at the office and realized the importance of switching off at the end of the day.

Practice Acceptance

The concept of acceptance is one we struggle with the most. This is because we feel that accepting that we cannot finish the work in a day or that we won't attend to something immediately is a sign of weakness. On the contrary, knowing what you can achieve during your working hours is a strength. This is why you need to accept that working longer hours does not allow you to achieve more. You might be able to impress your colleagues or clients initially, but you will not be able to maintain these long hours continuously. It is better to know what you are capable of and impress them by being able to produce quality results consistently.

You need to practice this acceptance daily. Not responding to work after hours does not make you weak or less productive than others. It enriches your life by providing work/life balance and makes you more productive during working hours. You have to remind yourself that work is continuous, it never ends. Stopping at the end of your work day is not going to change that fact.

Being able to unplug and switch off from work when working from home is an important lesson to learn. It is best that you practice it consistently in order for it to become a habit. Otherwise, it is easy for the lines of work and home to blur when there is no physical separation between the two. Working from home is, in part, a way to know yourself better as a worker. Whether you work as a remote employee, run your own business, or split your time between home and the office, you will begin to understand yourself better. It will be easier to evaluate your productivity levels and time management skills without outside interference and influence. As a result, you will be able to identify which areas you need to work on.

The six steps provided in this book will help you address the aspects that are crucial to working from home. Each step takes you through building a firm foundation that will enable you to hone your time management skills and maximize your productivity. They also feed into each other in a way that gives you a fully integrated plan. Thus, by creating a designated workspace, you will be able to minimize distractions and give yourself the time needed to develop a schedule and set goals, knowing your strengths. In doing so, you will achieve better productivity during working hours and be able to unplug at the end of the day, knowing you have achieved your work-from-home goals.

Conclusion

Working from home either permanently or via a hybrid situation post-pandemic has become a popular option for employees and companies across the globe. This is because they have both realized the benefits with regard to cost savings and productivity. Although, there are some people who battle to adapt to this change due to a number of reasons. The lack of social interaction, the disruption of daily routines, and the increased number of distractions at home can make you feel like working from home is not the right decision. However, when you know how to effectively manage your time when working from home, you will soon discover that it can be done easily and in a way that gives you the balanced life that you have always dreamed of.

In order to achieve effective time management at home, you have to be willing to try new things and be willing to learn more about yourself. That's one of the key advantages of working from home—you will discover your strengths and also what conditions are needed for you to be productive. These are sometimes unclear when working from an office because there are so many elements that overshadow them. Working from home will give you a clear indication of what contributes to your productivity and what hinders it. Before I started looking at ways to help me work from home efficiently, I just thought a workspace would be wherever I sat down with my laptop. I never knew how much a dedicated workspace would change the way I worked until I tried it out!

This is why I wanted to write this book for others navigating the world of working from home. I wanted to provide you with steps that can be implemented quickly that will ensure that you get the positive outcomes you desire over time. As I've mentioned a few times now, working from home is a learning experience. Once you implement these steps, you have to work on them to optimize them for your unique situation. This will ensure that you are always improving based on what you learn about yourself and your working style.

The first step of creating your ideal workspace is key to enforcing all the other steps that follow. This is because when you step into your workspace, you effectively leave your home life behind, and it becomes your distraction-free zone. It allows you to retain your focus and let others at home know that you are unavailable. In turn, this minimizes the majority of home distractions. However, you can also follow the tips in chapter two that will help you avoid distractions and temptations while working from home. In doing so, you will find that you actually have more time to work during your working hours.

This extra time can then be utilized more effectively by developing a schedule that helps you plan ahead and stay motivated. A schedule when working from home is an essential time management tool. It not only decreases the number of decisions you have to make in a day but allows you to also decrease the amount of time spent looking for documents or requesting information. Every element of your schedule will help you effectively use your time and eliminate any form of distraction because everything is accounted for, including breaks. This way of working will also give you an opportunity to set clear goals that you can clearly track and measure. You will find it much easier to reach your goals when working from home because you have a much clearer path established. This clear path, coupled with your improved productivity, will enable you to successfully reach your goals and set new ones. As a result, you can enjoy constantly improving yourself by setting new challenges that will further develop your strengths.

This is what the fifth step of effectively managing your time when you work from home addresses. You have to learn your strengths and work on them further to improve yourself. There is no use focusing on your weaknesses because it tends to demotivate you to look at flaws. However, by focusing on your strengths, you can achieve new heights and set larger goals that will continuously move you forward and keep you motivated. The sixth and final step is what is necessary for you to maintain a healthy and balanced lifestyle when working from home. This is also a crucial step of time management and one that often gets left behind. Without this step, the others will not work because you will be too tired to maintain your productivity during working hours. In addition, I found that working long, extended hours made me miss my true potential when I initially started working from home. I was still productive, but my constant state of anxiety and tiredness made me miss some major opportunities and prevented me from seeing better solutions. Now when I work, there's a clear plan and a defined endpoint to my work day. The mental clarity that this provides makes a huge difference during the day, and my energy levels are also better sustained. It makes working from home so much more effective and enjoyable. Who wouldn't want to say that when speaking about work?

You can achieve a healthy work/life balance when working from home while still maintaining high levels of productivity. The trick is to effectively manage your time and factor in both work and home life. It may seem like a challenge at first, but this book has given you the methods to put you on the track to success. You just need to input the dedication needed to implement them. I am certain that you will see results as I am still experiencing them every single day. I look forward to hearing about your results using the methods outlined in this book, so be sure to let me know in the reviews. Working from home is a journey, and I hope that this book has given you a clearer path to continue on!

References

Aguinis, H., Gottfredson, R. K., & Joo, H. (2012). Delivering effective performance feedback: The strengths-based approach. *Business Horizons*, 55 (2), 105–111.

Apollo Technical. (2021, January 5). *Statistics On Remote Workers That Will Surprise You*. Apollo Technical LLC. https://www.apollotechnical.com/statistics-on-remote-workers/

Apollo Technical. (2022, April 12). Surprising Working From Home Productivity Statistics. Apollo Technical LLC. https://www.apollotechnical.com/working-from-home-productivity-statistics/

Becca. (2020, March 19). *What Should My Work from Home Schedule Look Like?* Halfhalftravel.

https://www.halfhalftravel.com/remote-work/work-from-home-schedule.html

Chai, C. (2021, July 12). *How Blue Light Affects Your Sleep.* Everyday Health. https://www.everydayhealth.com/sleep/blue-light-what-is-it-and-how-does-it-affect-your-sleep/

Chua, C. (2014, May 9). *11 Simple Tips to Effective Email Management.* Lifehack. https://www.lifehack.org/articles/productivity/11-simple-tips-effective-email-management.html

Doran, G. T., Miller, A., & Cunningham, J. (1981). There's a S.M.A.R.T. way to write management's goals and objective. *Management Review, (AMA FORUM),* 70(11), 35-36.

Duffy, J. (2018, September 10). *The 10 Best Note Taking Apps in 2018.* Zapier. https://zapier.com/blog/best-note-taking-apps/

Expert Panel. (2021, April 23). *Council Post: Working From Home? Eight Tips To Schedule Your Day For Maximum Productivity*. Forbes. https://www.forbes.com/sites/theyec/2021/04/23/working-from-home-eight-tips-to-schedule-your-day-for-maximum-productivity/?sh=3d2f62f70e0a

Five Ways to Identify Your Personal Strengths and Apply Them to Project Work. (2019, May 23). LiquidPlanner. https://www.liquidplanner.com/blog/5-ways-identify-personal-strengths-apply-project-work/

Glenn Dutcher, E. (2012). The effects of telecommuting on productivity: An experimental examination. The role of dull and creative tasks. *Journal of Economic Behavior & Organization*, 84(1), 355–363.

Greg. (2021, April 5). *What Is The Best Ergonomic Desk Height? | Why Does It Matter?*. Control Physical Therapy. https://controlphysicaltherapy.com/what-is-the-best-ergonomic-desk-height/

Gruman, G. (2020, September 24). *How to set up a work-from-home "office" for the long term.* Computerworld. https://www.computerworld.com/article/3545478/how-to-set-up-a-work-from-home-office-for-the-long-term.html

Hill, B. (2020). *The importance of unplugging while working from home during the COVID-19 pandemic.* Wthr.com. https://www.wthr.com/article/news/local/the-importance-of-unplugging-while-working-from-home-during-the-covid-19-pandemic/531-d74df874-7ab2-4f9d-9921-82b120ef284f

How to unplug after a day working from home. (n.d.). Robert

Walters. https://www.robertwalters.com.au/career-advice/how-to-unplug-after-a-day-working-from-home.html

Kassmeier, E. (2020, October 12). *3 Benefits of Knowing Your Strengths.* Zaengle.com. https://zaengle.com/blog/benefits-using-strengths-work

Kunesh, A. (2019, March 11). *Your To Do List and Beyond: 8 Powerful Ways to Manage Your Tasks.* Zapier. https://zapier.com/blog/task-management-strategies/

Mark, G., Gudith, D., & Klocke, U. (2008). The cost of interrupted work: More speed and stress. *Conference on Human Factors in Computing Systems - Proceedings.* 107-110. 10.1145/1357054.1357072.

Mendoza, N. F. (2021, March 31). *Distractions and the downsides to working from home.* TechRepublic. https://www.techrepublic.com/article/dis

tractions-and-the-downsides-to-working-from-home/

Miniano, M. (2020, May 21). *Here's How Your Outfit Can Improve Your Mood While Working From Home.* TripZilla. https://www.tripzilla.com/dress-up-work-home/110181

Newton, C. (2020, May 21). *Mark Zuckerberg on taking his massive workforce remote.* The Verge. https://www.theverge.com/2020/5/21/21265780/facebook-remote-work-mark-zuckerberg-interview-wfh

NERIS Analytics Limited. (2022). *Free personality test.* 16Personalities. https://www.16personalities.com/free-personality-test

Nguyen, T., Reinert, M., Hellebuyck, M., & Fritze, D. (2019). *2019 Mind The Workplace.* Mental Health America.

https://www.mhanational.org/research-reports/2019-mind-workplace-report

Page, M. (n.d.). *Avoiding Distractions While Working from Home*. Michael Page. https://www.michaelpage.com/advice/career-advice/growing-your-career/avoiding-distractions-while-working-home

Patterson, R. (2020, May 1). *8 Project Management Apps to Keep Your Team Organized in 2021*. College Info Geek. https://collegeinfogeek.com/project-management-app/

Prodoscore. (2020, May 19). *Prodoscore Research from March/April 2020: Productivity Has Increased, Led By Remote Worker*s. Www.businesswire.com. https://www.businesswire.com/news/home/20200519005295/en/

Robalino, S. (2019, March 4). *13 Home Office Upgrades You Need If You Work from Home*. Ambition & Balance. https://blog.doist.com/home-office-upgrades/

Rosen, S. (2020, September 3). *Here's How Much Money You Really Save by Making Coffee at Home*. Time. https://time.com/nextadvisor/banking/savings/save-money-by-making-coffee-at-home/

Sococo. (2020, September 2). *The Top 5 WFH Distractions (and How to Conquer Them)*. https://www.sococo.com/conquering-wfh-distractions-remote-work/

Sorenson, S. (2014, February 20). *How Employees' Strengths Make Your Company Stronger*. Gallup.com. https://www.gallup.com/workplace/2316

05/employees-strengths-company-stronger.aspx

Spawn, L. (2020, January 9). *Council Post: Four Strategies For Setting Measurable Goals In A Remote Work Environment.* Forbes. https://www.forbes.com/sites/forbeshumanresourcescouncil/2020/01/29/four-strategies-for-setting-measurable-goals-in-a-remote-work-environment/?sh=3f8c76553014

Succeed at WFH: How to Plan and Stick to a Work Attire. (2022, March 10). Jobstreet. https://www.jobstreet.com.sg/career-resources/plan-your-career/5-reasons-why-a-work-from-home-dress-code-is-important/

Suner, E. (2020, February 6). *Council Post: Why Leaders Should Focus On Strengths, Not Weaknesses.* Forbes. https://www.forbes.com/sites/forbescoachescouncil/2020/02/06/why-leaders-should-focus-on-strengths-not-weaknesses/?sh=6fe5cf203d1a

Wiest, B. (2015, November 24). *12 Daily Routines Of Famous People In History – And What You Should Take From Each.* Thought Catalog. https://thoughtcatalog.com/brianna-wiest/2015/11/12-daily-routines-of-famous-people-in-history-and-what-you-should-take-from-each/

www.ingramcontent.com/pod-product-compliance
Lightning Source LLC
Chambersburg PA
CBHW071502220526
45472CB00003B/883